TEXAS MISSIONS

TEXAS MISSIONS

NANCY HASTON FOSTER

Lone Star Books®
An imprint of Gulf Publishing Company
Houston, Texas

LONE STAR GUIDE:
TEXAS MISSIONS

Lone Star Books®
An imprint of Gulf Publishing Company
P.O. Box 2608 ☐ Houston, Texas 77252-2608

10 9 8 7 6 5 4 3 2 1

Library of Congress Cataloging-in-Publication Data

Foster, Nancy Haston.
    Lone Star guide—Texas missions / Nancy Haston Foster.
        p.   cm. — (Lone Star guides)
    Includes bibliographical references and index.
    ISBN 0-89123-035-1 (alk. paper)
    1. Spanish mission buildings—Texas—Guidebooks.
    2. Historic buildings—Texas—Guidebooks.   3. Texas—Guidebooks.
    4. Texas—History, Local.   I. Title.   II. Title: Texas missions.
    III. Series.
    F387.F68   1999
    917.6404'63—dc21   98-49241
                                                                   CIP
Printed in the United States of America.

Printed on acid-free paper (∞).

Front cover photo of Mission Concepción © Laurence Parent.

Back cover photos of Mission San José walkway © Laurence Parent and entrance © Christina Ybarra.

To my family,
who has always been there
with encouragement and support.

CONTENTS

ACKNOWLEDGMENTS

Thanks to these individuals and staffs of various organizations for their helpful information, research background, maps, and photos:

The Alamo and curator Wallace Saage
Felix Almaraz, Jr.
Catholic Diocese of El Paso
Daughters of the Republic of Texas
El Paso Convention & Visitors Bureau and Jutta Matalka
El Paso Mission Trail Association and Sheldon Hall
Santiago Escobedo
Robert Espinosa of Southwest Parks & Monuments Association
Goliad County Chamber of Commerce
Goliad State Historical Park
Institute of Texan Cultures
C. J. Long, former Alamo curator
Mission Tejas State Historical Park
Herbert C. Morrow
Old Spanish Missions Historical Research Library
Presidio La Bahía and Newton Warzecha
San Antonio Convention & Visitors Bureau
San Antonio Missions National Historical Park (National Park Service) and Alan Cox and Rosalind Rock
Texas Parks & Wildlife Department and Jerry M. Sullivan
Tigua Indian Reservation and Marty Silvas
James W. Ward
Bob Washington

EXPLORING THE MISSIONS

THE SURPRISINGLY WILD AND WOOLLY MISSIONS ... WHERE THE TEXAS FRONTIER BEGAN

Don't let the missions fool you. They may look religious and historic and all that. But rake off some of that pious, historic dust and you'll find some elongated Texas tales that rate up there with giant armadillos and one-riot/one-Texas Ranger yarns.

And they'll all be true. Intrigue, battles, Indian raids, plagues, starvation, you name it, and the missions lived through it. A sort of pre-urban *As The World Turns* that spanned the Spanish missionaries fighting to survive on the hostile frontier in the 1600–1700s to the battles of the Texas Revolution in the 1800s—the latter sometimes literally in mission front yards.

So while our Texas missions are beautiful religious architectural specimens to be viewed and revered, don't forget the adventurous people behind them. All of this makes for engaging family outings.

Where else could you find such flamboyant combatants and players as Davy Crockett, Jim Bowie, Santa Anna, Indians, Spanish conquistadores, padres, and both Mexican and Texan revolutionaries, all rolled into one package? Yes indeed, this book includes the **Alamo**, which was a mission in its first Shirley MacLaine life, long before its famed battle in 1836.

Visit the missions for their patined Spanish Colonial architecture and get a fun, painless dose of Texas' florid history at the same time. And learn how the southwest's real estate (in that new country on the block, the United States) was settled and won by the Spanish, for a while anyway. Some of the missions are even combination parks where you can camp out or hike. (The San Antonio Missions National Historical Park has no camping, but does have picnicking and hiking trails. The two state parks with missions have both camping and recreational facilities.)

See a Spanish cannon up close and personal, and peer out from a bastion where it guarded the walled compound. Walk the trails missionaries walked. View religious sculpture and Indian (Native American) hunting tools. Many archeological digs have been done at mission sites, and the

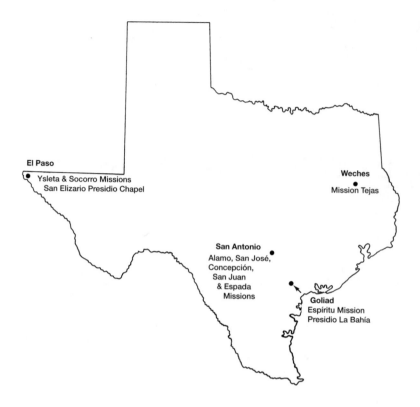

El Paso
● Ysleta & Socorro Missions
San Elizario Presidio Chapel

Weches
●
Mission Tejas

San Antonio ●
Alamo, San José,
Concepción,
San Juan
& Espada
Missions

Goliad
Espíritu Mission
Presidio La Bahía

artifacts are on display. Too, see how even Texas ranching began with the missions. Without the early Spanish mission ranches, there would have been no King Ranch or J.R.'s Southfork.

These activities and more are available at some of the missions. This guidebook will clue you in to what you should look for and where, so that you'll get the most out of the missions and nearby sites.

QUICK OVERVIEW OF MISSION HISTORY . . .
WHERE THE ACTION WAS AND WHY

This book will also provide you with some of the latest colorful revelations about elusive mission history. Archeologists and historians are constantly puttering around ruins and archives to unturn some new fact or artifact that will unravel a past mystery or debunk some myth. That's why historical markers aren't very reliable—they're written in granite. State and national park researchers and academics don't necessarily agree among themselves either on what *really* happened at the missions and when. It's a fascinating puzzle with new pieces falling into place continually.

For a little background, remember that these bucolic churches, these bastions of Christianity, were at times in their history hotbeds of frontier adventure, rivalry, and warring cultures. They were the sites of that historical soap opera where nations vied for empires, gold, and trade. In the seventeenth and eighteenth centuries, Spain used her missions as geographical pawns to increase her share of the New World real estate. That the tenacious Franciscan missionaries who founded them also happened to spread Christianity and civilization, well, that was just lagniappe.

The missions were again a center of action when the nineteenth century rolled around. This time it was Mexico who battled and won its independence from Spain, only to have Texas in turn fight for its freedom from Mexico's tyrannical rule. The Republic of Texas used the missions, already built like forts, as strongholds in the struggle to free itself from Mexico, which considered Texas a substate, just as the Spanish had.

The Alamo, or Mission San Antonio de Valero, is the most well-known example of a church-turned-fort and the site of the bloody conflict whose outcome engendered a battle cry known the nation over—"Remember the Alamo!"

But there was another, lesser-known yell that resulted from a battle in the vicinity of another Texas mission and La Bahía presidio near Goliad. There, the Texan forces under Col. James Fannin lost again and ended up imprisoned in La Bahía presidio, with about 342 of them being massacred. Thus the cry "Remember Goliad!" arose to inspire the Texans also.

So you can see, the erratic history of Texas' early frontier days and subsequent civilization can be traced by simply visiting and studying the missions.

To portray the missions in their heyday as always bustling with activity would be grossly inaccurate, for at times, they were dull, tranquil, and lonely outposts. Still, once the first missions were founded in Texas in the 1680s (you'll see later that a few historians speculate that one mission was even started in the 1630s), they became the centers of colonization and thus the center of the action. For missions *were* the frontier, and their inhabitants suffered all the inherent problems of living on the frontier—starvation, drought, floods, plagues, and Indian attacks.

Missions were Spain's means of colonizing the land it had explored in the New World. Presidios, or forts, were usually built nearby to protect them, and this system had already worked in Peru and Mexico.

Since the Catholic church and royal government were intertwined, the missions were subsidized. Being beneficial to both the church and state, they served as a way of subduing the native culture, while utilizing free labor. Thus, the missions were religious and trade schools all rolled into one, used for teaching the Indians how to farm, ranch, weave, and build, while providing them with food and shelter.

While some Indians (Native Americans) welcomed these advantages, others resented this cultural intrusion and were less than eager converts. Slavery is more like it, say some Native American historians. There were frequent Indian attacks, and the missionaries were constantly having to retrieve recalcitrant runaways. But to Spain's credit, its colonization system at least provided for the original Americans. Other systems weren't so hospitable.

From the 1500s when Spaniards Cabeza de Vaca, Coronado, Moscoso, and Oñate set foot in Texas, Spain began extending its territory of New Spain northward beyond Mexico to surpass the other European powers, England and France, which were already entrenched in eastern North America.

This weather-beaten, sculptured stone entrance is the doorway to Texas' most historic lodestone, the Alamo.

Spain resented France in particular, which had become interested in the Mississippi River area and landed in Texas by mistake in 1685 (La Salle). Thereafter, Spain settled and built missions near Indian villages and rivers to protect her territorial claims. From these settlements grew familiar Texas towns such as San Antonio, El Paso, Goliad, and Nacogdoches, and the rugged highways that connected them, known as El Camino Real (The King's Highway), provided a system of routes that is still used today.

Thus Spain left a large, undeniable footprint on the Texas landscape. Those dedicated Franciscan missionaries, along with the military and civilian settlers, brought with them ranching and irrigation systems, a legal system, and a colorful language, all of which still exert a profound influence on the Texas culture.

Another legacy left us by the Spanish missionaries is the endearing mission architecture itself. These fine old Spanish colonial churches (most still Catholic parish churches today) give a comfortable, patined texture of antiquity to the state. When viewing the missions, remember that those old walls reverberated with not only ecclesiastical chants, but Indian yells and war whoops. Not only used for holy rituals, these missions have also been cattle pens, army headquarters, private residences, and mercantile stores. A lot of humanity has trundled through them over their centuries-old existence, and it's this motley cast of characters and their arresting tales that make the missions unfailingly intriguing.

HOW TO USE THIS BOOK

This book is designed to give you quick reference to the missions. Each mission section begins with pertinent information including address, phone number, days and hours open, and admission fees, if any. "W" indicates wheelchair accessibility. Next is a discussion of the mission, pinpointing its uniqueness and telling you what to look for in the way of slide shows, films, museums, and recreational and picnicking facilities. Detailed subsections are arranged to allow you to read as little or as much as you wish about topics such as history, archeological digs, architecture, and restoration. You will find specific directions on how to get to each mission as well as a map, a special events calendar, and a description of what to see nearby.

You will notice that the missions are grouped by geographical regions, beginning with San Antonio (because this area has the most missions). Finally, you will find a general overview of the history of Texas missions and a look at the frontier life in them.

SAN ANTONIO MISSIONS

San Antonio, the place where fun-seeking vacationers and convention-eers alike love to set boot in, is also prime Texas history territory. You can almost get a cram course in history by just sauntering into the city and soaking up some Spanish Colonial and Texas history by osmosis.

As city spin doctors are apt to say, "We've got the Alamo and four other Spanish missions, more missions than any other city in the nation." 'Tis so. The famed Alamo was actually a mission to begin with, way before that renowned battle in 1836. And the four other missions now make up a national park, the San Antonio Missions National Historical Park.

How'd all this happen in San Antonio anyway?

Well, ever since Spanish padres and officials first happened upon the local river and named it San Antonio de Padua (after St. Anthony) in 1691, the area has been an arena for power struggles, battles, and political peccadillos. San Antonio itself was founded only a little while after New Orleans in 1718 and has a lively historical pedigree to match that of the Louisiana city.

The most well-known mission, the Alamo, anchors downtown San Antonio. Indeed, in the beginning it *was* San Antonio. It and the other missions sprang up, along with the presidio (fort), as a convenient way station to the older missions in East Texas, where Spain was attempting to protect its real estate from France. In time, the San Antonio missions would eclipse the ones in East Texas and become more successful, probably because they simply were closer to the headquarters of New Spain (in what is now Mexico) and because the Coahuiltecan Indians were more amenable to being "civilized." In fact, three East Texas missions had to be abandoned and relocated here (as Missions Concepción, San Juan, and Espada) because of bad relations with the Indians and the French.

The other mission here, San José, grew to become one of the flagships of the Spanish mission chain and is often touted as the "queen of the missions." Its architectural beauty and its large restored compound make it one of the best examples of a frontier Texas mission. After the Alamo, at least take in San José if you don't have time to see the rest.

THE ALAMO

Of course, before seeing any other Texas mission, you must see the Alamo. It is a whole story in itself. Though that saga is often embellished by tale-spinning Texans and free-wheeling novelists, it is enough to say that in 1836 a small, courageous band of men fought a bloody battle here and bought precious time for the fledgling Texas republic to later win its independence from Mexico.

SAN ANTONIO MISSIONS NATIONAL HISTORICAL PARK

The Alamo is conveniently located in central downtown San Antonio. From there, get a mission tour brochure and map from the Visitor Information Center across the street and make the tour of the other four missions by car. They are all located in south San Antonio, and Mission Trail signs point the way. The whole tour will take roughly a morning or an afternoon, but you might want to opt for a picnic lunch outside the missions grounds or at nearby parks. But get directions and use the map. Sometimes the Mission Trail signs are few and far between, and the routes to the last two farthest missions can be confusing. And remember, some routes and picnicking areas are isolated, so it's best to use precaution. To follow the Mission Trail signs from downtown, start driving south on S. Alamo Street where it intersects with Market Street (this point is a couple of blocks south of the Alamo). Continue on South Alamo, and you will begin to notice the Mission Trail signs that will lead you to the rest of the missions.

These four missions are run by the National Park Service and are officially called the San Antonio Missions National Historical Park. This is not your usual national park. The missions may be all in the same south San Antonio area, but they are strung out several miles apart at separate locations. And there are no camping facilities here. The Alamo is operated separately by the Daughters of the Republic of Texas. All are admission free and open daily.

There are other options for touring the missions. Several commercial bus tours leave from near the Alamo daily, and the public bus system (VIA) has a special cultural route going to the missions regularly during the day. See your hotel or the city's Visitor Information Center for details on costs and tour companies.

Don't forget the other sightseeing treats in San Antonio. This is tourist mecca, with both historical and recreational sites. See "What to See Nearby" in the section on the Alamo.

WHERE TO GET INFORMATION

Visitor Information Center

317 Alamo Plaza (across from the Alamo)
San Antonio, Texas 78205
(210) 207-6748 or (800) 447-3372

San Antonio Convention & Visitors Bureau

P.O. Box 2277
San Antonio, Texas 78298
(210) 207-6700

San Antonio Missions National Historical Park

Headquarters
2202 Roosevelt
San Antonio, Texas 78210
(210) 534-8833

Gray Line Sightseeing Tours

217 Alamo Plaza
San Antonio, Texas 78205
(210) 226-1706

VIA Metropolitan Transit (public bus)

800 W. Myrtle
San Antonio, Texas 78212
(210) 362-2020

THE ALAMO

Mission San Antonio de Valero

At Alamo Street and Houston Street, at 300 Alamo Plaza,
downtown San Antonio • Museum and Souvenir Shop
Open 9 a.m. to 5:30 p.m. Monday–Saturday; 10 a.m. to
5:30 p.m. Sunday in winter, until 6:30 p.m. in summer; closed
Christmas Eve and Day • Free • (210) 225-1391 • W

The Alamo. Just mention the word, and almost everyone's eyes, from
die-hard Texans to Europeans who don't even have crib sheets on American history, light up. The Alamo doesn't exactly suffer from lack of name
recognition. It has a high Q rating, as the media folks would say.

No wonder. Legends have been spun over the years about the famous
1836 battle, with Hollywood and John Wayne doing their part. And right-
fully so. The Alamo, where a band of about 189 (known) men died fighting
off a Mexican army of several thousand, *is* the stuff that legends and heroes
are made of. But lost in all this is the fact that the Alamo actually started out
life as a peaceful Spanish mission in 1718, which we'll go into later.

The Alamo's familiar facade has stirred the hearts of millions of visitors.

This old war-horse of Texas Independence wears well with time. Even today, in the midst of downtown San Antonio, surrounded by retail stores and bustling shoppers, the Alamo still stirs the heart of many a Texan seeing it and that bright red, white, and blue Texas flag flying proudly over it. In fact this is one of the most popular historic landmarks in the nation, attracting some three million visitors annually.

Passion, violence, and courage were found here in the men fighting for what they believed in, against hopeless odds. The Alamo saga *is* the narrative of rough-hewn men like Jim Bowie, Davy Crockett, and William Travis, who thought "Victory or Death" preferable to a Mexican dictatorship. Of course, the Mexican government held quite a different viewpoint; they took umbrage at upstart colonists wanting their country's land.

But this battle (actually it was a siege that lasted thirteen days; the battle itself lasted only about one and a half hours) played an important role in history. It bought time for Sam Houston to gather a make-shift army to defeat Santa Anna, the president-dictator who led the Mexican Army at the Alamo and later at the Battle of San Jacinto. That decisive victory brought Texas independence from Mexico in 1836.

Did you know that old Sam actually ordered the Texans to blow up the Alamo before they abandoned San Antonio, because he didn't think the mission could be defended? Fortunately, or unfortunately for the Texas defenders, they didn't pay any attention to him.

Once Texas got its freedom from Mexico, it was annexed by the United States in 1845. An ensuing border dispute resulted in the Mexican War (1846–1848), which gave America title to lands that eventually became Arizona, California, Colorado, Nevada, New Mexico, and Utah.

THE BATTLE OF THE ALAMO

What led to the battle of the Alamo? Well, basically it's the familiar story of people revolting against a tyrannical government.

Prior to 1836, Texas was an administrative substate of Mexico, and many Texas inhabitants were colonists from the United States accustomed to more democratic rule. These Texans did not care for President Santa Anna's dictatorship; they wanted to rule themselves.

The Mexican government felt otherwise and thought that the colonists should abide by the rules of the country whose land they inhabited. Since many adventurers and free spirits migrated to Texas, the stage was set for revolution.

A small clash at Gonzales, east of San Antonio, started things off in October 1835. About this time, Santa Anna sent his brother-in-law, General Martin Perfecto de Cos, to take command at San Antonio. Cos was soundly defeated by some Texan volunteers led by Ben Milam (hence the slogan "Who will go into San Antonio with old Ben Milam?") and sent packing back to Mexico.

This act infuriated Santa Anna, and he vowed to return to San Antonio to avenge the humiliating defeat. A most uneven grudge match was about to begin.

Why was it so uneven? Many of the Texans who had captured San Antonio went home because they thought the fighting was over once Cos had surrendered and pledged never to fight against Texas again. Only about 100 volunteers remained at the Alamo.

The revolution was not an organized effort at this point, and only now was Sam Houston trying to muster an army of volunteers. Hearing that Santa Anna was amassing thousands of troops, Houston sent orders by his friend Jim Bowie that the Alamo's guns be taken and the walls blown up. Houston felt the Alamo could not be defended by so few men.

But Bowie didn't agree with Houston, and somehow the Alamo never got blown up. Shortly thereafter, William B. Travis, sent by Texas' provisional governor, Henry Smith, arrived on the scene, and there was a power struggle over command. But Bowie was sick with typhoid-pneumonia, and Travis ended up with the unenviable job of commanding an untenable defense.

(Santa Anna's siege of the Alamo began February 23, 1836, when his demand that the Texans surrender was answered with a cannon shot.) For twelve days the battle was mainly an artillery duel, because the Texans not only had more cannons than the Mexicans, but they also had sharp-shooters with better guns.

During the siege, Travis penned a famous letter carried out by courier Albert Martin to the town of Gonzales (Travis' letter became renowned later as its stirring contents were published in U.S. newspapers and the Texans' cause was told):

> Commandancy of the Alamo
> Bexar, Feby 24th 1836

> To the People of Texas and all Americans in the world—Fellow citizens and compatriots—I am besieged, by a thousand or more of the Mexicans under Santa Anna—I have sustained a continual Bombardment & cannonade for 24 hours & have not lost a man—The enemy has demanded a surrender at discretion, otherwise, the garrison are to be put to the sword, if the fort is taken—I have answered the demand with a cannon shot, & our flag still waves proudly from the walls—*I shall never surrender or retreat.* Then, I call on you in the name of Liberty, of patriotism & everything dear to the American character, to come to our aid, with all dispatch—The enemy is receiving reinforcements daily & will no doubt increase to three or four thousand in four or five days. If this call is neglected, I am determined to sustain myself as long as possible & die like a soldier who never forgets what is due to his own honor & that of his country—

> VICTORY OR DEATH
> William Barret Travis
> Lt. Col. Comdt.

Travis had already requested help from Colonel Fannin and his Texan troops at the Goliad garrison, but to no avail. Desperate, he sent another courier. Again Fannin failed him, having started out with several hundred men but turning back. Only the town of Gonzales answered the call, sending 32 men and boys, who slipped in between enemy lines.

On March 5, the Mexican cannon bombardments became so threatening that Travis called together his men and gave them the choice of fighting or trying to escape. Legend has it that he drew a line on the ground with his sword and asked all who would stay at the Alamo to cross it. Only one man, Louis Rose (nicknamed "Moses") is thought to have bucked peer pressure and sneaked out.

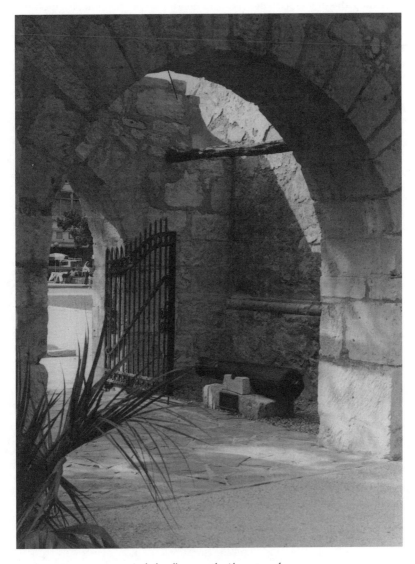

Arched walkway on the Alamo grounds.

Let it be noted that some historians debate whether Travis really drew a line or that this Rose was actually at the Alamo at all. This and other facts about the Alamo siege and battle are often debated among scholars and history buffs. Sometimes, new documents and eyewitness accounts are turned up over the years to shed new light on what happened. This leads to back-and-forth haranguing among historians on which varying accounts to believe. After all, even eyewitness accounts of present-day auto fender-benders most always vary, because that's the nature of people's recall. So can you imagine how hard it is to pin down what happened over 150 years ago?

The next day on March 6, the assault came around dawn. With bugles sounding the dramatic "Deguello" (no quarter to the defenders), the Mexicans attacked on several fronts. But it wasn't till they regrouped and hit the north wall that they succeeded in penetrating the Alamo's defenses.

After only about 1 1/2 hours, the battle was over, for how long could 189 men hold out against an estimated 1,500 to 2,500 Mexican troops? The number of troops for both sides is still debatable, but the Alamo staff has been able to identify 189 Texan defenders (which included a handful of Tejanos, or Texans of Spanish and Mexican descent) who died in the battle. They use the 189 figure as the number of total defenders in the Alamo. Some historians, however, point to Mexican battlefield accounts saying there was a body count of around 250 Alamo defenders. It's been estimated that the Mexican forces amassed in San Antonio totaled from 3,000 to 4,000, with the previously mentioned smaller numbers actually participating in the battle. Any way you look at it, these were pretty poor odds for the Alamo defenders.

Naturally, historians also disagree on other points, such as who died where and how. Many say that the defenders all died during their defense of the Alamo compound. Travis fell across his cannon with a shot through his forehead; Bowie died on his cot. Some historians, however, think that a few of the defenders were captured at the end of the battle and summarily executed under Santa Anna's orders. An estimated 600 were killed on the Mexican side during the battle.

Most people think nobody on the Alamo side survived the battle. But that isn't so. At least thirteen noncombatants are known to have survived, mainly women and children. And there may have been two Alamo defenders, one dying from his wounds later, who somehow managed to escape the dragnet of the Mexican Army and General Santa Anna. The General sent one of the Texan survivors, Susanna Dickinson, wife of Captain Almeron Dickinson, to spread the word of the Alamo's demise to the Texans.

Mrs. Dickinson was in a room in the church when the Mexicans came in during the fighting. She related that they killed two little boys and ". . . I saw four Mexicans shoot [a man named] Walker and stick their bayonets into his body and raise him up like a farmer does a bundle of fodder with a pitchfork when he loads it onto a wagon."

Santa Anna had the Texans' bodies piled high and burned in a pyre.

Probable layout of the Alamo walled compound, much larger at the time of the 1836 battle. Note that the square was in front of the church (shrine) or to the west on into what is now Alamo Plaza. (Courtesy of C. J. Long).

The Cast of Characters

Some of those who came to Texas were already well known before the battle immortalized them. The following are capsule biographies of the most renowned heroes of the Alamo, including the Texans' flamboyant foe, General Santa Anna.

James Bowie was a Tennessean and about age 40 when the battle took place. A hard-drinking Indian fighter famous for his Bowie knife, he had married Ursula Veramendi, daughter of the Vice Governor of Mexico, but lost her to cholera several years before the battle.

David Crockett, also from Tennessee, was 49 when he died at the Alamo. He was renowned for his marksmanship and always called his rifles "Betsy." He also presumably wore the infamous coonskin cap. A frontier Tennessee legislator and three-time U.S. Congressman, he has in more recent times been immortalized in song as "Davy" Crockett.

William Travis, a lawyer by profession, came to Texas under mysterious circumstances. He was said to have killed a man, perhaps his wife's lover. A womanizer himself, Travis was quite a romantic and a writer of profuse prose. He was the commander of the Alamo at age 26.

General Antonio Lopez de Santa Anna (you can see why he's called Santa Anna for short) was a pompous general, who also happened to be the President of Mexico. He had a fetish for opium and the ladies and called himself "Napoleon of the West."

The Mission Era

Although most famous as a battlefield, the Alamo has led nine lives, spanning several centuries. It's been everything from a fort and hospital to an Army depot and mercantile store selling groceries and booze. But it began as a peaceful mission in 1718, a date the city of San Antonio calls its founding date.

Mission San Antonio de Valero, as it was originally called, was founded more or less as a halfway station for the Spanish on their way to missions in East Texas from Mexico. The route these missionaries took was the beginning of El Camino Real (The King's Highway), later called the Old San Antonio Road to East Texas.

A Spanish expedition of officials, soldiers, and friars first stumbled on the area in 1691. They named it and the local river San Antonio de Padua, because they made their discovery on that saint's day. They found the Payaya Indians already living there in the river valley.

Later, a Franciscan missionary, Fr. Antonio de San Buenaventura y Olivares, requested and received permission to establish a mission in the newly discovered San Antonio area. Told to relocate the failing San Francisco Solano mission, which was near what is now Eagle Pass, to this new area, Fr. Olivares did so and renamed it San Antonio de Valero. (The Valero part shrewdly honored the Viceroy of New Spain, the Marquis de Valero.)

Fr. Olivares first set the mission up on the west bank of the San Antonio River near San Pedro Creek, a little northwest of the mission's present location. It was moved in 1719 to the east bank of the river and then again in the 1720s to its present location, upstream. It served as a mission to the Indians until 1793 when it became the first Texas mission to be secularized. Most of the state's missions had begun to fail, and the Catholic Church began to close them down. Therefore, San Antonio de Valero's lands and tools were parceled out to the Indian inhabitants.

At its peak period as a mission, in the 1740s and 1750s, the Alamo had about 328 Indian inhabitants; a farm and an acequia to irrigate the fields; a ranch with cattle to the northeast; textile, carpenter, and blacksmith shops; a granary; a friary; and a chapel. The church part that we recognize today was begun in 1758, though it was never fully completed.

THE ALAMO'S OTHER LIVES

After the Catholics closed down the mission, a Spanish cavalry unit from Alamo de Parras in Mexico occupied the abandoned compound in the early 1800s, and people started calling the place El Alamo (*alamo* means cottonwood tree). About this time the old friary at the Alamo was also used as San Antonio's first hospital, treating both soldiers and civilians. Later came the Mexican troops who used the place as a fort, and in 1836 the Texas revolutionists made their heroic stand there.

After the famous Battle of the Alamo, the place lay vacant a few years, until the Republic of Texas deeded it back to the Catholic Church. But again it reverted to military use when the Church leased it to the Army in 1847 as a quartermaster depot. The Confederates took it over during the Civil War, and then it was occupied by the U.S. Army until 1876 when the Army moved to the new Fort Sam Houston.

About this time, a merchant by the name of Honore Grenet bought the property with the friary (or long barrack) on it and added a frame second story. In this august historic site, he sold groceries, dry goods, boots, whiskey, tobacco, and produce. He also leased the old Alamo church from the Catholic Church to use as a warehouse!

Following Grenet's death, a notice about his estate offered the store property for sale, together with its lease of the Alamo, by proclaiming:

> The location on Alamo Plaza . . . with the street cars passing it every few minutes during the day and until late at night makes this one of the most eligible business sites in San Antonio. This property will prove to be a Genuine Bonanza to its purchaser or lessee.

Well, the Hugo and Schmeltzer Company couldn't pass up this bonanza, and they turned the barrack into a department store. Fortunately, the

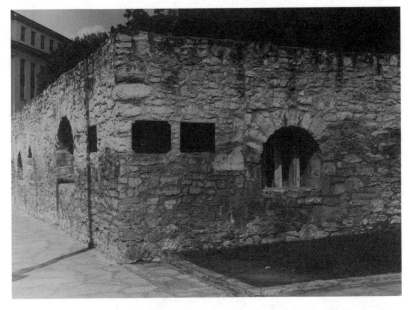

These outer walls of the Alamo compound encompass the Long Barrack, which earlier served as the convento where the friars stayed.

State of Texas finally stopped some of this nonsense and bought the church part from the Catholic Church in 1883. However, the enterprising businessmen hadn't given up on the commercial value of the property with the long barrack. In 1903, they tried to turn it into a hotel site. Clara Driscoll helped the Daughters of the Republic of Texas forestall this event by buying the property herself and letting the state repay her later. (Adina de Zavala, a DRT chapter president, had led the fight to save the site.) The state then gave custody of the whole property to the DRT to be maintained by them at no charge to the state—which they have done ever since. Thanks to them and Clara, we don't have an Alamo Hotel on the Alamo grounds.

ARCHITECTURE AND RESTORATION

In its heyday as a mission, the Alamo was situated much differently than it is today. It had a walled square typical of Spanish missions, but it wasn't the one you see around the church today. Instead of enclosing the church, the walls were built in front of it to the west. The church was just an adjunct to the *convento patio and convento* (now the long barrack), which faced on the square.

The missions, as mentioned earlier, were used by Spain to colonize the area, giving the Indians both religious instruction and skill training. Each had to be a self-supporting unit, and the Mission San Antonio de Valero was no exception. The compound included the aforementioned carpenter, blacksmith, and textile shops (the Indian women wove their own fabrics and clothes). And there were rooms built into the walls of the square for the Indians to live in.

The earliest structures were simply huts of adobe and straw. Later on, more permanent structures of native stone were added, though many buildings of adobe were still used. All of these disappeared through deterioration, battles and time. The only original structures left now are parts of the church and convento, and even these have undergone changes.

The present church structure was begun in 1758. It was never completed before the mission was shut down in 1793. The Spanish cavalry unit that was later stationed in the abandoned mission in the early 1800s (and gave the mission its current name) put a roof on the church. But this was removed by General Cos in 1835 when he was fortifying the Alamo. He piled the debris from the roof against the back wall and used it as a dirt ramp to roll cannons up on.

The big battle of 1836 didn't help the Alamo's architecture any either. It was left to the new lessee, the U.S. Army, in 1849 to restore the convento and rebuild and reroof the church. The credit for the distinctive curvilinear gable top of the front facade goes to Major E. B. Babbitt, who was in charge of the restoration. The Army also added the two upper windows.

It wasn't until the 1930s under the aegis of the DRT that the church's vaulted ceiling and roof were installed. The DRT also acquired more of the property around the Alamo, and through the WPA the area was cleared, a wall surrounding the block added, and a museum built.

Now, for a little more detail on the Alamo's architecture: The church is cruciform in shape, with the two arms of the cross originally planned for side altars. The ceiling is vaulted, and there are side rooms for the sacristy, confessional, and baptistry. The floor is flagstone and the walls are of irregular stones (mainly native limestone). In short, the building is of simple design, with only the front facade having a decorative character. The front is called a retable facade, which like the altar of a church has niches to display statues and religious objects. It is in an early Baroque style, with floral designs and scalloped shell patterns surrounding the huge wooden doors.

While the Alamo may have the similar stone construction and the general Spanish colonial aesthetics of other missions, it really is atypical in that it has no bell tower.

ARCHEOLOGICAL DIGS AND FINDS

The Alamo has long fascinated archeologists, and in recent years they have uncovered a skull thought to be from one of the battle participants. It isn't known if it is a Texan or Mexican skull, only that it appeared to be that of a twenty-year-old male.

Over the years, the Alamo has been the site of many excavations, beginning with the one dug by the WPA in the 1930s in the area east of the church and the Long Barrack where there were commercial buildings. No records of their dig have been found.

Since 1966, archeological digs have been documented and the artifacts collected. Some of these (potsherds, musket and cannon balls, Spanish coins) have been displayed in the Long Barrack Museum.

Here's a brief list of the main excavations:

1966   The Witte Museum did excavations on the north side of the Alamo church in the convento patio areas. They uncovered the remains of perhaps the original north wall of the second patio or some other remnant of a structure in the North Court. Also in the Well Court, they found the remains of what appeared to be a room. The wall base was made of large adobe bricks.

1970   The Texas Archeological Survey excavated north of the DRT Library and uncovered nineteenth-century structural footings and part of the mission acequia.

1973   More excavations in the North Court were done by the Witte Museum. They uncovered the remains of what is believed to be the original walls of the convento patio and also of what appeared to be wall footings of four rooms.

1973   This dig by Thomas Hester of the University of Texas at San Antonio (UTSA) was east of the Museum/Souvenir Building and verified the location of the old acequia ditch.

1975   The Center for Archeological Research of UTSA excavated in the small park in Alamo Plaza, trying to locate the mission quadrangle south wall. The damaged remains of the wall footings were found.

1977   When the City repaved Alamo Plaza, its backhoe trenching just outside the front wall of the Long Barrack (convento) was monitored. It was determined that the present restored wall does indeed sit upon the original convento wall.

1977   Excavations were again carried out by the UTSA Center for Archeological Research when the City replaced the flagstone paving in front of the church. Datable cultural items retrieved from the stratified soil levels and the church's foundation were studied. Also a palisade ditch dug as a defense during the battle was discovered along with many battle artifacts.

1979–80   Probably the most intriguing item that has turned up is the skull found by the UTSA Center for Archeological Research team while digging near the wall in the North Courtyard. Tests indicate it is apparently the skull of an 1836 battle casualty. Found near musket balls and a gun lock, it belonged to a male of about 20, who probably died by the sword or a similar weapon. Excavations done on the west side of Alamo Plaza during River Walk linkage construction uncovered remnants of the old mission quadrangle west wall and rooms.

1992   Lone Star Archeological Services did excavations in preparation for installing a full basement under the Alamo museum/souvenir building. The whole dig area contained artifacts, including some Guerrero arrow points, but the site was so disturbed over the years that there was no stratigraphy. Some Colonial flooring was found to the east of the existing convento courtyard wall, suggesting early mission rooms in this area.

For archeology devotees, more detailed information can be found in reports published by the UTSA Center for Archeological Research on some of the more recent digs. The Museum/Souvenir Shop sells them.

TIMING YOUR VISIT

If possible, avoid seeing the Alamo when everyone else does, on weekends and holidays. It's a pleasant place for an outing anytime, but more so when the tourists aren't swarming. Naturally, summer is the big season.

How much time should you allow? You can easily go through the whole thing in an hour, but you should leave some time for sauntering around the landscaped grounds. This is the essence of San Antonio, being able to stroll in a green, tree-shaded area, listening to the birds sing, while surrounded by a teeming city.

Where do you go from here? You need only look on the side streets around the Alamo, particularly near the Menger Hotel. Tour buses and horse-and-carriages jostle for tourist business. Take one of the buses for a tour of the other four Spanish missions in the city, or drive your own car on the Mission Trail mentioned in the San Antonio introduction.

Directions to the Alamo

The Alamo is conveniently located in the middle of downtown San Antonio. Most of the freeways take you downtown, but the closest one to approach the Alamo from is on the east side of the central business district, and at this point is called both IH 35 and IH 37.

Get off on the Commerce Street exit and go west for three or four blocks until you reach Alamo Street, take a right on it, go north two blocks, and you're at the Alamo and Alamo Plaza. There is no special parking area—you'll just have to scramble for a meter or a commercial parking lot. But parking lots are plentiful and nearby, only a block or two away. Look for them to the northeast of the Alamo, an area less congested with stores and containing more parking lots. The Alamo occupies an entire block at Alamo and Houston Streets. Officially, it's at 300 Alamo Plaza.

Touring the Alamo

Free guided tours of the Alamo are given to the public daily, usually on the hour. They last about 30 minutes. Ask at the information desk in the church when the next one is scheduled, or do it yourself with their free map.

What to Do and See

Cenotaph

A gleaming white marble monument, dedicated to the Alamo heroes by the State of Texas in 1936, fronts the Alamo at the corner of Houston and Alamo Streets. This cenotaph was done by the sculptor Pompeo Coppini.

The Alamo Grounds

The Alamo today is a walled-in compound, taking up an irregular block in downtown San Antonio. After all, the mission was the original settlement, and the town grew up around it.

On the grassy, treed grounds are several buildings, the most obvious one being the former church with the familiar postcard facade associated with the Alamo. Along with the Long Barrack Museum walls, the church is the only original part of the Alamo left standing, and much of it had to be restored. The other buildings, the Museum/Souvenir Shop, the Daughters of the Republic of Texas Research Library, and the meeting hall, have been added in more modern times. They are constructed, however, to blend in with the aged look of the original Alamo structures.

The Daughters of the Republic of Texas are the patron angels of the Alamo. They've been taking care of it for the State of Texas, at no cost to taxpayers, since 1905. And they don't charge visitors either; admission is free. One way they support their effort is through selling giftshop/tourist items.

The DRT keeps the place spick-and-span, and colorful flowers and plants bloom year-round. These landscaped grounds are a pretty place to

Present layout of the Alamo grounds.

stroll downtown even if you aren't interested in history—particularly on a sunny day. There is usually a breeze. Besides the carefully manicured flowers, there is one area of cactus and yucca to remind you what a part of Texas outside of San Antonio is like: rough-hewn, prickly country where only arid plants survive.

If you want to rest your peds, there are benches throughout the grounds, particularly by the separate restroom area at the back of the block complex on the northeast wall.

Kids, who don't know the word "rest," usually find the Cavalry Courtyard (on the northwest corner) interesting for all the Spanish cannons located there to touchy-feel. One, a carronade, has a plaque reading: "This cannon was used in the battle of the Alamo. Probably on the west wall. It was made inoperative by General Santa Anna before he left for San Jacinto. This type of cannon was made in Scotland in the 1790s."

Another area kids gravitate to is the acequia, or narrow irrigation canal that flows behind the Alamo church and gift shop/museum buildings. The reason? The big goldfish swimming away. This irrigation ditch is part of the original one built to supply the Alamo when it was Mission San Antonio de Valero in its earlier life.

Shrine, Museum, and Exhibits

All three public buildings on the Alamo property have exhibits. The former church has a few exhibits tastefully scattered about, but it still retains its somewhat hallowed atmosphere.

After taking an obligatory picture of the front of the Alamo (the trick is not to include ten strangers walking by), enter the church, or the "Shrine" as the DRT likes to call it.

Church

It's not quite as quiet as a library, but things are more subdued in here. After all, it was a church. (No photos are permitted inside.) Inquire at the information desk about the free guided tours that last about 30 minutes. If you want to tour it on your own, ask for a map guide sheet and mosey around the exhibits—they are pretty self-explanatory.

The small room to the right as you come in the front entrance is the baptistry; the one to the left is the confessional. The larger rooms to the left were probably the sacristy. Now they are called flag rooms because they contain flag exhibits.

Around the church walls are display cases with interesting little items like Crockett's wallet and his rifle "Betsy," and a Bowie family knife. There is also a long rifle (called the Dickert rifle after its maker) actually used in the defense of the Alamo, as well as a model of the Alamo as it appeared in 1836. Paintings of Davy Crockett, William Travis, James Bowie, and James Bonham hang on the walls.

Long Barrack Museum

After viewing the exhibits in the church, go out the back door, take a left, and walk past the big tree and Convento Garden courtyard. Now you're coming to the Long Barrack building, also part of the original structures left to posterity. Besides being used as the obvious—a fortress—in the earlier mission period, it was the living quarters for the priests. Now it's called the Long Barrack Museum. In it, you'll find well-done exhibits on early Indians, the Alamo's early mission period, the battle, and the Texas Republic.

First off, take in the short, 15-minute color movie offered continually during the day in the end room of the Long Barrack building. Narrated by local historian Henry Guerra, the movie is free and gives an easy, palatable overview of the Alamo's history, from Spanish missionary days on to the famous battle.

The entrance to the Long Barrack Museum is in the middle. This is a small museum, with several rooms of attractive graphic displays showing enlargements of historical pictures, maps, and diagrams, plus text panels and assorted glassed-in exhibits of pertinent historical memorabilia.

From time to time, museums may change their exhibits around, as does the Alamo. Here's a mention of what this museum is currently displaying as of this writing. To begin with, there is a display on the first Texans, the Payaya Indians, who lived in the San Antonio River valley and called the area Yanaguana. Next is one on the Alamo's life as a mission and the other surrounding missions in San Antonio. Then, there's an early settlers display, showing the Canary Islanders and Texas patriots such as Juan Seguin and José Navarro.

The Gone to Texas display is about people who emigrated to Texas when Mexico encouraged colonization there. Stephen F. Austin, long considered the "father of Texas," was one of them, as was James Bowie. Shown nearby are a Bowie knife, and flintlock and percussion rifles. Then, the museum has the men of the Alamo, including William Barret Travis, the commander. Another of his letters is mentioned. This one, written during the siege on March 3, 1836, after his more famous earlier one, was to Governor Smith in which he said, ". . . victory will cost the enemy so dear, that it will be worse for him than defeat." This turned out to be pretty prophetic.

The Fall of the Alamo display goes into more detail about the battle, telling what happened each of the 13 days of the siege and showing both Mexican and Texan clothes. (In another room at the time of this writing were exhibited Mexican General Santa Anna's ornate ceremonial robe and the fancy brass folding travel cot he used to sleep on, presumably in his tent—definitely not a man who would have been content with Motel 6 accommodations.) There is a list of the Alamo heroes and a large model of the Alamo compound as it was at the time of the battle.

Displays on the Goliad Massacre and the victory at San Jacinto for Texas independence follow, including Sam Houston's engraved cane and sword and a religious medal taken from Santa Anna when he was captured. Finally, there's an exhibit on what it took to save the remains of the Alamo in later years and who helped to spearhead it—Adina de Zavala and Clara Driscoll.

The Long Barrack Museum houses archeological artifacts and Spanish and Texas Republic era items.

Museum/Souvenir Shop

Next on the agenda is the combination museum/souvenir shop, which you'll be facing when you exit the Long Barrack Museum. It's across the Cavalry Courtyard, the building east of you. Historic exhibits are mainly in the middle of this large room. Books and souvenirs are for sale on the fringe. Don't miss the large model depicting the battle scene at the Alamo on March 6, 1836. This differs from the models seen in the Alamo church and Long Barrack Museum. It shows hundreds and hundreds of tiny Mexican soldiers surrounding the Alamo compound and climbing the walls to fight the few Alamo defenders, and is all in scaled detail down to the ladders, trees, cannons, animal pens, etc. The plaque says it was created by Thomas F. Feely, Jr., and best of all, it gives you a feel for the whole expanse of the battle and the site. Kids and adults alike find it fascinating.

Other exhibits here show guns (from Colt army to Derringer pistols), Sam Houston memorabilia (another cane and his razor), and Texas pioneer lifestyle (barbed wire samples).

As for souvenirs, obviously this is Alamo likeness heaven. Some of the merchandise is quite nice, some of it Texas kitsch—from fine, color historical map reproduction posters that even the most snobbish of interior decorators wouldn't mind using, to T-shirts and buckles with the Alamo on them. Whatever your heart or pocketbook desires. There are Bowie knife replicas that look very real and dangerous. You wouldn't want to meet up in a dark alley with anyone, including Jim Bowie himself, carrying one of these. Or the ubiquitous Davy Crockett look-alike coonskin caps that kids

The Alamo's landscaped grounds make for a pleasant downtown stroll. The Museum/Souvenir Shop is in the background.

love. Inflation has even caught up with the Alamo. A Davy Crockett wooden nickel costs 15¢.

Daughters of the Republic of Texas Research Library

This pleasant library of the Daughters of the Republic of Texas is open to researchers, not the browsing public. Located on the south side of the Alamo complex, it has books, maps, documents, manuscripts, periodicals, clippings, and photographs pertaining to Texas history, in particular the era of the Texas Republic. Photographic reproduction and duplication services are available.

Refreshment Break

No food and drink are allowed in the buildings, and none are for sale there. But there are soda machines outside the restrooms building, or you can go out to Alamo Plaza in front of the Alamo and buy an ice cream bar or raspa (snow cone) from street vendors. Unfortunately, sometimes there have been too many entrepreneurs hawking their goods to tourists and cluttering up pretty Alamo Plaza. You can eat in one of the several fast-food places across the street, or for a more pleasant meal, take your taco or sandwich in the fresh air of Alamo Plaza with its old-fashioned gazebo, park benches, and shade trees. You will find yourself sitting in the lap of history, for even the merchant and hotel buildings around the Plaza are old. (The venerable Menger Hotel dates from 1859.) There are, of course, many restaurants in the area within a block or two.

ANNUAL EVENTS

Since the Alamo practically has to beat off visitors with a stick, there are no festivals held here. And too, because the DRT doesn't like to overcommercialize the historic site, most of the events that take place at the Alamo are serious, patriotic ceremonies. But now and again, a bit of frivolity slips in, such as at Fiesta time when the city has a ten-day celebration around April 21 (San Jacinto Day, when Texas won its independence from Mexico in 1836).

Here are some annual ceremonies:

March 2

Texas Independence Day ceremony—This commemorates the day Texas declared its independence from Mexico.

March 6

Heroes Day—This is the solemn observance in the church of the day the Alamo fell to Santa Anna's troops in 1836, with the DRT honoring the heroes who died with a roll call of the defenders' names. Also on this same memorial day, the San Antonio Living History Association reenacts parts of the battle siege in front of the Alamo on Alamo Plaza. Members are all decked out in costumes and uniforms of the period to represent the Alamo defenders and the Mexican Army. They fire cannons and rifles and wave swords, and usually quite a crowd of onlookers enjoys all of this. The Living History Association has various activities for the public during the week around March 6.

March 17

St. Patrick's Day—Harp & Shamrock Society of Texas has a wreath-laying observance with accompanying music and celebration.

Week Surrounding April 21

Fiesta—This ten-day celebration includes many activities, but those involving the Alamo are:

The Coronation of King Antonio, which takes place in front of the Alamo at night, with a lot of pomp and frivolity as the King of Fiesta is crowned amidst torchlight.

The Pilgrimage to the Alamo, which is an afternoon processional parade that ends up at the Alamo to present floral offerings in honor of Texas heroes.

November—Friday after Thanksgiving

City Christmas Tree Lighting—Christmas starts early with the annual tree lighting celebration on Alamo Plaza, in front of the Alamo. BIG, BIG tree gets lit with the Alamo and evening lights providing a picture-card background. Holiday music.

FUTURE PLANS FOR ALAMO PLAZA

Periodically, various San Antonio and Texas citizens, historians, and politicians debate about changing the Alamo and its environs to enhance it for tourists and posterity, and sometimes their own agendas. Alamo Plaza, which fronts the Alamo, is often the target. The Alamo's site is complicated by the fact that the town grew up around it, in all its urban splendor and unsplendor (including nearby streets possibly covering ancient mission burial grounds for American Indians). In the process, the old mission compound and walls (also there for the battle of 1836), which were originally projected out into present day Alamo Plaza, are no longer there or visible for visitors to see how large the original battle site or compound was. As of this writing, the city is looking at what now are only suggestions to somehow enhance Alamo Plaza's historic nature and/or reconstruct the original walls and compound. This would be no small project, costing millions to raze or move present buildings. There are, of course, a lot of restored buildings' owners, some preservationists, and others who oppose fooling with the intimate character of the entire plaza and Alamo that took years to evolve and attracts three million visitors annually.

Downtown San Antonio is brimming with historic sites and entertainment areas. The River Walk, just a couple of blocks to the west, is a must-see. Shops, sidewalk cafes, and art galleries line the bustling San Antonio River as it winds its way through town. You can take a barge ride down its one-and-a-half miles of landscaped parkland.

Quaint La Villita (village), HemisFair Park, the Institute of Texan Cultures, San Fernando Cathedral, the Spanish Governor's Palace, and Market Square, are all within walking distance or a ride on the motorized VIA city streetcar. All these sites are well worth seeing, but if you want to keep your base of operations near the Alamo, there's more than enough to keep you out of mischief. About half a block away to the southeast is San Antonio's answer to the trendy mall, Rivercenter. Only it's in a U-shape with an arm of the San Antonio River in the middle. You can shop 'till you drop or chow down at the fast-food court and restaurants.

Just across the street from the front of the Alamo is a combination Ripley's Believe It or Not and Plaza Theatre of Wax, if you go in for this sort of thing. Also, you'll find a delightful hodgepodge of new and old retail stores in renovated storefronts, from upscale art galleries and funky stores to pizza and ice-cream parlors.

For information on these sights, simply cross the street to the Visitor Information Center in the 300 block of Alamo Plaza.

Alamo Movie at IMAX

For a really big close-up encounter with the story of the Alamo, try the IMAX Theater's movie, *Alamo . . . The Price of Freedom*. The IMAX is located in Rivercenter Mall, and its screen is six-stories tall, ten times larger than regular movie screens. The movie is a 45-minute docu-drama which tells the tale of the Alamo defenders. Stereo. Shows daily at intervals. Admission. Gets pretty full-up during tourist season, so you may want to go by and pick up tickets ahead of time for a later showtime.

City Tours

Various commercial conveyances with guides eager to show you the rest of the city are easily found on the Alamo's doorstep. Several bus lines offer long-range city and mission tours, and streetcars and horse-and-carriages will take you for a spin in the downtown area. All depart daily, some every hour on the hour, during the day from near the Alamo. For more information on tours, contact the Visitor Information Center.

SAN ANTONIO MISSIONS NATIONAL HISTORICAL PARK

MISSION SAN JOSÉ

Mission San José y San Miguel de Aguayo

3200 block of Roosevelt Avenue at Napier, San Antonio
Large grounds with visitor center, exhibits, bookstore, and gift shop
Open daily 9 a.m. to 5 p.m.; closed Thanksgiving, Christmas Day and
New Year's Day • Free • (210) 932-1001 • W

Mission San José is the classic archetype of a Texas mission with its graceful, patined Spanish Colonial architecture. See it, if none else. Nationally renowned, it's the state's largest mission compound and has the most ornate church facade. Here, you'll get a feel for the rugged, frontier days of the 1700s and how the resolute Franciscans built primitive oasis cities in the wilderness.

Life was severe then. If backbreaking hours of hard labor didn't shorten your life, marauding Indians or epidemics would. And this large restored mission compound in south San Antonio is one of the few left to reflect the fort-city nature of these outposts.

"A veritable fortress" is what one friar called San José in 1749. "Although greatly exposed because of its location to attack by the Apaches, who have become so daring that they threaten the Presidio of San Antonio even in the daytime, they have never bothered the mission." The whole square of walls has been restored, with the church ensconced in the middle, and there is even a mill nearby.

The chapel's beauty and ornate craftsmanship stand out incongruously in what must have been a harsh, sparse environment when the mission was founded in 1720 shortly after the Alamo. Although the phrase "Queen of the Missions" has been effusively overused, San José is indeed the foremost Texas mission and one of the most magnificent in the country. As such, it's the cornerstone of the San Antonio Missions National Historical Park and one of the most photographed missions.

The classic lines of the church's bell tower, combined with the ornate exterior stone sculpture, hark back to an era when artisans had the time to hone their craft. On a sunny day, there is nothing more inspiring than the sight of this aged Spanish colonial church, with its off-whites highlighted by the sun, contrasting with the bright blue Texas sky.

Absorb a bit of the peaceful serenity of long ago while standing on the square's flat prairie ground. Never mind the occasional traffic or jets overhead; the mission complex is still far enough away from urban hustle to give you an idea of what secluded pioneer life was like then.

San José can be seen in an hour easily, but why pass up a chance to luxuriate in this ready-made serenity? Spend half a day, and take a lunch (or buy one at the various fast food restaurants across the street) and picnic on the grounds (allowed only in the amphitheater area north of the mill). An indoor refreshment room with vended snacks and cold drinks is also on the north square wall.

Usually the staff gives guided tours periodically during the day. But you can also pick up a map at the visitor center and follow the square to the Indian quarters, granary, official residences, mill, church, sacristy (with its famous, legendary "rose window"), and courtyard convento, and then go back by way of the corner bastion, to see the unique way residents had of defending the walls. You'll see how the Indians lived in their apartment-like quarters, with their crude tools and utensils. Typical of most missions, there were carpenter, blacksmith, tailor, and textile shops, as well as nearby farmlands and a ranch, called El Atascoso, some 25 miles away to the southwest near the present-day towns of Poteet and Pleasanton. Have your walking shoes on—the square is almost two football fields long. First, take in the exhibits and movie at the visitor center. Among the exhibits is a large model of the mission (circa 1770s).

San José is still a parish church, and if you have a chance, take in the colorful mariachi noon Mass on Sundays. The mission is also the site of colorful special events during the year, all open to the public. For instance, there are the July 4th parish festival and the presentation of the Christmas pageant, Los Pastores, in the Christmas season.

Life in a Frontier Mission

What was it like to live in the missions on the cutting edge of the frontier? How was a mission set up, and how did it work? One way to visualize San José then is through the eyes of a visiting church fireman, Fr. Juan Agustin Morfi, who made a report on Spain's frontier missions and toured San José in 1777.

It "is in truth, the first mission in America, not in point of time, but in point of beauty, plan, and strength, so that there is not a presidio along the entire frontier line that can compare with it," he wrote. (Thus San José's "Queen of the Missions" claim.)

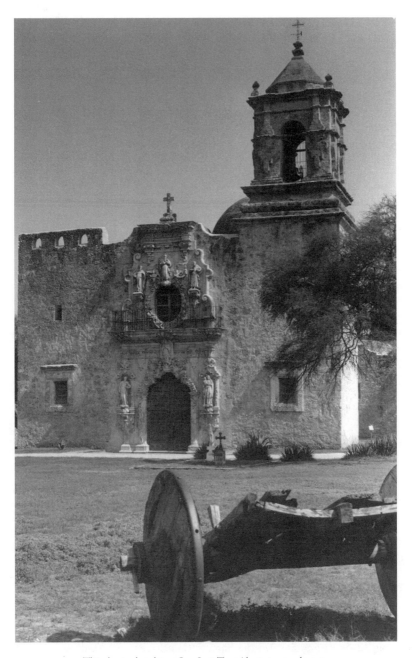

This classic chapel is at San José, Texas' largest restored mission.

". . . no one could have imagined that there were such good artists in so desolate a place." Everything ". . . is in such good order and so well-planned, that even if the enemy would be able to lay siege to the mission, the besieged, having their granary well-filled with food and plenty of good water in their wells, could afford to laugh at their opponents."

San José in that era appeared much as we see the restored compound today. Along the square walls were the Indian "apartments" that consisted of one room and a kitchen with a fireplace. These had crude cots covered with buffalo hides and blankets woven by the Indians. As Morfi described the place further: "There is also a loom in which rich blankets, cotton, cloth, sackcloth . . . are woven. There is a carpenter shop, a blacksmith shop, a tailor shop, and everything needed in a well-regulated community." The granary was on one side wall, with the church and convent inside the square. An acequia or irrigation ditch flowed through the square. Outside the walls was the mission farm. It "occupies an area about a league square and is all fenced . . . For its benefit water is taken from the San Antonio River and distributed by means of a beautiful irrigation ditch to all parts of the field, where corn, beans, lentils, cotton, sugar cane, watermelons, melons and sweet potatoes are raised . . . and there are some fruit trees . . .," continues Fr. Morfi.

And even farther away, perhaps 25 miles to the southwest, (near present-day Poteet and Pleasanton) was the mission ranch, El Atascoso. All the San Antonio missions had ranches of their own, and this was probably the largest. At least it seemed to have the highest count of livestock—1,500 head of cattle and 5,000 sheep one year.

HISTORY

San José did not have the turbulent history of, say, the East Texas missions, which Spain had to abandon because of border hostilities with the French. In contrast, San José has led a more sedate life, allowing, however, for routine pestilence and Indian raids. No major battles were fought in its confines, though U.S. troops barracked there in the mid-1800s did use the lovely church facade for target practice!

San José was founded in 1720 at the behest of Franciscan Friar Antonio Margil de Jesus. The friar was an astute fellow who asked the governor of Coahuila-Texas, Marques de Aguayo, for permission to establish the mission and named it after him. Margil, in charge of several East Texas missions, had to abandon his missions there and flee to Mission San Antonio de Valero (the Alamo) as a temporary refugee. While in San Antonio, he decided that Spain could use another mission in the area to act as a way station to the East Texas missions when they were reestablished.

San José's earlier sites on the San Antonio River were slightly north of here, somewhere near where Mission Concepción is today. Temporary huts and adobe structures acted as its "buildings." It wasn't until a move to the present site on the west bank that permanent structures arose. There is a report that by 1749 the stone granary was finished. It still stands today and is thought to be one of the oldest remaining stone buildings in all of

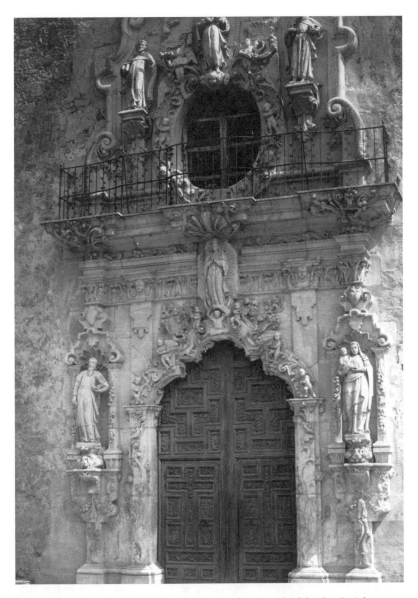

Pictured here is some of the delicate stonework at the church entrance that led to San José's being dubbed the "queen of the missions."

Texas. It even predates the Concepción church and the Spanish Governor's Palace. Construction on the present church (an earlier stone chapel predated it) didn't begin until 1768 and wasn't completed until the 1780s.

The mission, which at one time had a peak Indian population of 350, was partially secularized in 1794, and part of its property was distributed to the Indian residents. By 1824 it was completely closed down as a mission, though it continued to be used for church services.

It was downhill for the mission after this. Texan and U.S. troops occasionally quartered here at various times in the 1840s–1850s, and a monastery used the place for about eight years in the 1860s. But slowly the mission compound fell into ruin. The Indian quarters and walls disappeared. Parts of the church walls collapsed, and eventually so did the dome.

It would take until the 1930s for San José to be restored. In 1941 it became a State Historic Site and then in 1983 part of the National Historical Park.

ARCHITECTURE AND RESTORATION

Don't be misled by the mission compound as you view it today. Only a small portion of all these old-looking structures is actually *original*. Much of the compound is just good reconstruction work. But such a good cosmetic job was done that all the reconstruction blends in well, appearing to be weathered and several centuries old. By the 1930s when most of the restoration was done, only part of the church itself (its dome, roof, and some walls had collapsed), some of the convento arched walls, the granary, and the lower part of the mill were left standing.

Thanks to the tenacious San Antonio Conservation Society, which spearheaded the mission's revival by buying the old granary property in 1930, the community got behind the restoration project and utilized county, church, and private monies to fund it. WPA labor was used.

The church's dome and roof, as well as the square walls around the compound, which had completely disappeared, had to be reconstructed. The church doors had been stolen, and tourists could even buy chunks of the crumbling structures as souvenirs!

Many people, not just the friars who had a vested interest, have acclaimed the San José chapel as a prime example of Spanish colonial style. It has a square bell tower on the right of the ornate stone sculptured entrance, a barrel vaulted ceiling, a cupola roof, and other clean, classic lines. Depending upon how much sun is out, the church may appear different colors. Made of limestone from a quarry near Mission Concepción, San José appears to be greyish-white when there is little sun. With more, it becomes cream-colored.

The baroque entrance has lavish sculptured stonework and a retablo—including religious figures, cherubs, and scrolls topped by a window balcony and cross. Naturally, San José (St. Joseph), the patron saint of the mission, has a prominent top place in it. All this elaborate stonework frames the large carved wooden doors. The church exterior is thought to have originally been colorfully frescoed with geometric designs of bright yellows, reds, and blues. Some reconstructed samples of these frescoes are on the south side of the church.

The graceful sacristy window, also on the south side of the church, has been the subject of much conjecture and many local tales. The window has grillwork in the middle surrounded by ornate stone-carved scrolls and

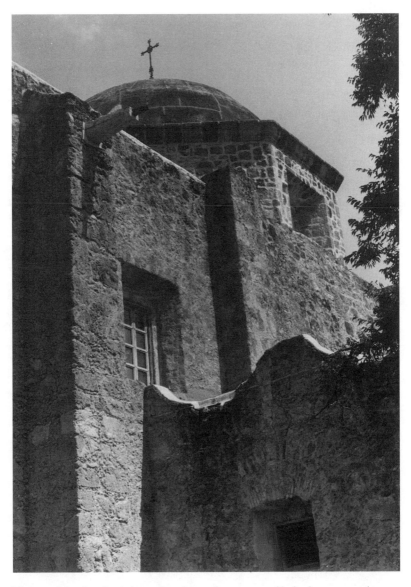

The original San José church dome collapsed due to deterioration and had to be reconstructed in the 1930s.

foliage, and for years has been locally referred to as the "rose window." But architects insisted that it did not have the rose pattern of a true rose window, so someone suggested that artisan Pedro Huizar sculpted this while pining away for his lost love Rosa—and they called it Rosa's window for a while. However, researchers still debate it and don't know who did the window.

Contrasting with the ornate entrance, but continuing with the overall simple design of the church, the inside worship area has off-white walls

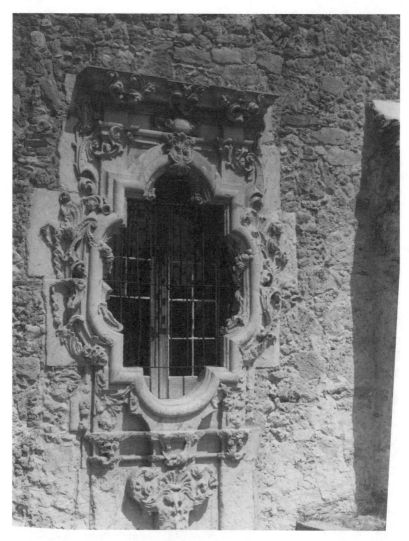

Sacristy window (legendary "rose window"), with its ornate stonework, is one of the mission's land-marks and is located on the south side of the church. Tales about the window abound.

with brightly colored trim and a lack of busy ornamentation. There are wooden pews, rock floors, and candle-shaped wall light fixtures. The high, vaulted ceiling is taller than the chapel is wide. And the church doesn't follow the traditional cruciform shape either. The sacristy is on the south side and opens back to the remaining arched walls of the convento and the cloister garden.

The convento was both living quarters and offices for the missionaries. The same Fr. Juan Agustin Morfi mentioned earlier told us more about the

Mission San José

1 Church	12 Bastion	23 Hornos
2 Sacristy	13 Office	24 North Wall Returns
3 Convento	14 East Gate	25 Foundation Remains
4 Convento Garden	15 Southeast Gate	26 Mill and Millrace
5 Granary	16 Southwest Gate	27 Kilns
6 Colonial Carpentry Shop	17 West Gate	28 Vat
7 Gift Shop	18 Composanto	29 San Jose Acequia
8 North Wall Indian Quarters	19 Garden Well	Madre
9 East Wall Indian Quarters	20 East Well	
10 South Wall Indian Quarters	21 South Well	
11 West Wall Indian Quarters	22 West Well	

convento in 1777, when he wrote that it was: ". . . two stories with spacious galleries. There are enough rooms for the missionaries and for the convenience of a few guests, as well as the necessary offices for the religious, a large and well-ordered kitchen, a comfortable refectory and a pantry. There is an armory and a room where decorations and dresses are kept for the various dances that are held with the mission."

Behind the church and north wall is an old gristmill built sometime around the late 1700s by a Father Pedrajo. The lower level was uncovered in 1933, and the top restored by Ernst Schuchard. It was a gristmill of the Norse type, with the turbine wheel in the chamber below.

Be sure to note the corner bastion at the southeast corner of the square walls. The bastion was built in a bulbous shape so that defenders could survey the two exterior walls and fire on attackers through wall holes. This was a standard feature on Spanish defensive structures. No wonder the Apaches gave up trying to storm the mission compound itself and resorted to attacking stragglers outside.

DIRECTIONS TO SAN JOSÉ

Mission San José is in south San Antonio. If you are only going to visit it and not take the Mission Trail from downtown to all four of the missions, get on IH 37 going south and exit west on Southcross Blvd. (This intersection is a bit confusing if you are coming from downtown San Antonio. You actually exit onto New Braunfels, then take a right on Southcross.) Continue westward on Southcross until you reach Roosevelt. Take a left and go south on Roosevelt until you reach the 3200 block, where it intersects Napier. Turn left on Napier, and the visitor center and parking lot will be immediately on your left.

If you wish to take the Mission Trail route, see the map and instructions at the beginning of the San Antonio section. If you'd rather take a bus, the city bus line (VIA) offers a special express route to the mission, with many departures daily.

TOURING SAN JOSÉ

The park entrance and visitor center are at the southeast corner of the mission. You have a choice of joining one of the park staff guided tours, which are usually given periodically daily, or taking your own self-guided tour. Several commercial sightseeing buses also tour San José; check near the Alamo, where they leave daily.

To take the self-guided tour, get a free map from the visitor center and prepare for a lot of walking. The tour directs you around the square, with a detour on the north side to the mill outside the walls. There are explanatory plaques at each point. Look for these areas, generally indicated on the map:

- Indian quarters—These consisted of two rooms, with a fireplace in one corner. Rawhide cot, pottery, and crude cooking utensils are displayed.

- Outdoor oven—called a *horno*, this was reconstructed by the WPA. Ordinarily made out of adobe.

- Water well—Original wells were hand dug.

- Granary—At the northwest corner of the compound, it could store 5,000 bushels of corn and other produce. The granary predates the church.

- Colonial carpentry shop—Near the granary. Inhabitants had to do all their own carpentry, blacksmithing, etc., and this area could have housed different types of work over the years.

- Acequia (irrigation ditch)—This was the Acequia Madre or primary irrigation ditch of San José. The water was tapped at a dam on the San Antonio River and channeled to the two and one-half square miles of mission fields nearby.

- Mill—The upper millworks include the hopper, grinding stone, and controls, with the turbine below. Water powering the mill was brought by the acequia, then channeled to the crop fields. The plaque says "oldest mill in Texas," but remember that only the lower part is thought to be original; the upper is reconstructed.

- Kilns—Conical pits at the mill's side are believed to have been pottery kilns.

- Processing pit—There has been supposition that this was a syrup cooker.

The granary at San José (circa 1749) was one of the few original structures of the mission to survive time's erosion.

This view of the San José church is from within the huge pastoral walled-in compound.

- Church and sacristy—See "Architecture and Restoration" section. The sacristy, used to store vestments and religious service items, is the only part of the compound that never collapsed.

- Sacristy window ("rose window") and restored frescoes—These are on the south side of the church. See "Architecture and Restoration."

- Convento and courtyard—The convento served as living quarters and offices for the Franciscan missionaries. All that remains are the Roman and Gothic arches and walls.

- Indian soldiers' quarters—Indians trained in defense lived near the corner bastions. They had to keep watch for Apache Indian attacks.

- Corner bastion—Defenders could survey the two exterior walls from here and fire on any attackers. See the info display on Spanish mission defense.

- Fortified gate—Platforms above the gates were used for defense, and the loopholes in rooms on each side enabled viewing and firing on unfriendlies.

- Mission Decline and Restoration exhibit—Photos and text about San José's decline and ultimate restoration.

Visitor Center

A large visitor center greets you near the southeastern corner of the mission. It houses a large seated theater where you can view a film about south Texas history, and see assorted exhibits, maps, and artifacts. A more recent addition to the mission complex, the modern center is built of sandstone and designed to give a low profile and not detract from the mission itself. And rightly so, the aged mission is the main billing here. The park service staff gladly answers your questions, and some books are also available at the center.

Bookstore and Gift Shop

There is a fine bookstore, a joint effort of the Southwest Parks and Monuments Association and the San Antonio Missions National Historical Park, which is stocked not only with books on Spanish colonial mission history, but also on Indians, San Antonio, and Texas. Air-conditioned, it is a welcome respite from summer heat and a pleasant place to browse.

The gift shop, near the northwest corner, is above-average too. Oh, you've got some of the usual trinkets and gewgaws, like armadillo items (which seem high on all Texas merchandisers' Top Ten charts for some reason), but the shop sells some pretty nice things that you really wouldn't mind giving as gifts, such as silver jewelry, handwoven items, clothes, folk art, and prints of the missions. Naturally, there are umpteen items with the mission motif.

Special Events

Every Sunday at noon

Mass—A colorful mariachi Mass is held at the church.

July 4

July 4th Festival—This is an all-day parish festival open to the public, with mariachi entertainment, food, and game booths. There is no admission charge.

December (one evening)

National Park Open House—One evening (dates vary) in December, the National Park plays open house at San José, with candles (luminarias) lighting the way and free refreshments. They usually try to pick an evening with something happening astronomy-wise so the skies can be observed. Free.

Late December or early January

Los Pastores—This Christmas pageant is traditionally held on one Saturday evening shortly after Christmas. But the dates may vary. The celebration begins with Mass at the church, followed by the centuries-old Spanish Christmas play. Local parishioners perform outdoors in brightly colored costumes and masks, with the church as a setting. Los Pastores means "the shepherds" and was used by Franciscans to teach the Indians about the Christmas story while throwing in a good/evil plot to boot. Sponsored by the San Antonio Conservation Society (224–6163), it also includes music

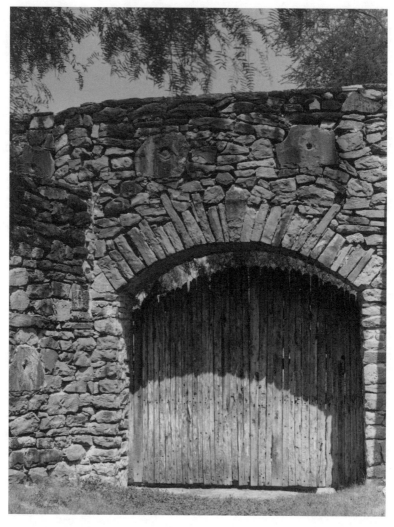

This is the fortified southeast gate in the walls, which were built in a square shape to enclose the mission compound.

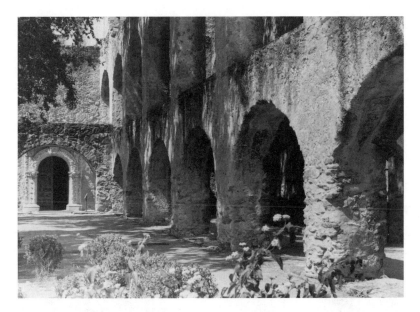

Shadows play on the remaining arched walls of the old convento.

and food booths with traditional Mexican goodies such as buñuelos (delightful crispy sugared pastry in the shape of a tortilla), hot chocolate, and tamales. The play is performed in Spanish with an English narration. Dress warmly; it's usually cold this time of the year. Free.

MISSION CONCEPCIÓN

Mission Nuestra Señora de la Purísima Concepción de Acuña

807 Mission Road at Felisa, San Antonio • Open daily 9 a.m. to 5 p.m.; closed Thanksgiving, Christmas Day and New Year's Day • Free (210) 534-1540 • W

Mission Concepción lays claim to being one of America's oldest unrestored stone churches. Unlike most missions whose walls and innards have crumbled over the years, Concepción was made so well it's still basically the same church it was when built in 1755. And like other Texas missions, this one also played a minor part in the Texas Revolution. A skirmish between the Texans and Mexicans, dubbed the Battle of Concepción, took place nearby.

You'll find Concepción first on the Mission Trail if you're touring the four missions in south San Antonio after seeing the Alamo first, and it is the closest to downtown. From here follow the Mission Trail signs south to the other three missions, all four of which embody the San Antonio Missions National Historical Park.

After seeing the bustling Alamo, Concepción (short for Mission Nuestra Señora de la Purísima Concepción or Mission of Our Lady of the Immaculate Conception) will seem sedate. Much less commercialized and much quieter, it is near an older workingman's neighborhood. But that's the charm of Mission Concepción. As you drive up, the rolling expanse of green grass and trees sets off the simple majesty of the church standing there. It makes for a good photo op, both outside and inside. The stone church is typical of mission design, with two towers and a cupola. Symmetrical and chaste, it has a dash of embellished sculptured stone around the large patined wooden doors at the front entrance. This simple parish

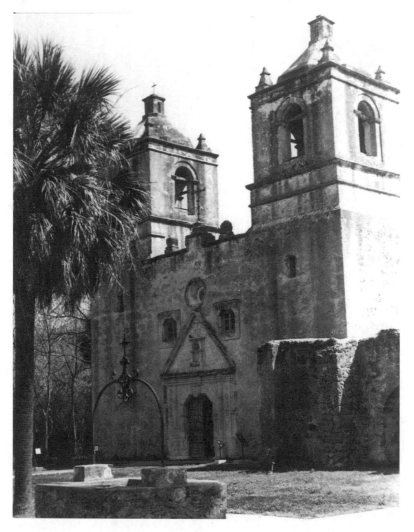

Concepción church was built so well in about 1755 that it never crumbled into disarray.

mission church is also beautiful in its simplicity inside. Sit a while on the wooden pews and contemplate before you leave.

Something unusual to look for at this mission are the remnants of frescoes, colorful interior wall paintings frequently done in the mission era. None remain at the other park missions. One of the frescoes to be on the lookout for is what they used to call "God's Eye," because it peered down at you and presumably kept the missionaries and parishioners out of mischief.

The original square, including the wall and Indian quarters, is long gone, as is the granary. But the convento, the living quarters of the missionaries, is still there.

Park in the parking lot and go into the nearby small, modern national park building to get information and inquire about the informal tours usually given periodically during the day. From the park building, follow the sidewalk and pass by an old well that has never gone dry. From this point walk along the sidewalk to the church. Inside is a real delight for people who like unadulterated design. Plain, white walls are slightly accented by bright colors of teal, mustard, and maroon. Inexpensive wooden pews face up to the altar, which is covered by a Moorish dome touted for its acoustics. From here, walk into the sacristy to the right; then upstairs to the "Father President's office" to gaze at the compound below. Next, tour the convento, also attached to the church. Here's where to look for the restored frescoes.

Concepción, still a parish church today, started out as a mission in 1716 in East Texas and was eventually moved to San Antonio in 1731. But its history after the mission period is even more vivid. Mexican revolutionaries holed up here, those Texas revolutionists we mentioned earlier fought nearby, the U.S. Army used it as a camp, and once it even was utilized as a cattle pen! In 1898 Teddy Roosevelt trained his Rough Riders nearby.

You can see the mission complex in as little as thirty minutes, if you don't linger.

HISTORY

Concepción has had what you might call a vagabond history, since it was one of the three missions moved to San Antonio in 1731 from East Texas. One of the first missions built by the Spanish among the Tejas tribes, Concepción was established in 1716 near present-day Douglass in Nacogdoches County. But when the nearby protective presidio was shut down due to cost cutting, the missionaries requested that they be allowed to move the three missions to a safer area. The missions were moved in 1730 to a location in central Texas on the Colorado River. For some reason this site didn't work out, and the missions soon moved to the San Antonio River in 1731. Moving was no small feat, considering the distance, and required carrying church furnishings across big rivers, not to mention the herding of the cattle, horses, mules, and burros.

Concepción was set up on its present site, which is a little east of the San Antonio River and about two and a half miles from the Alamo, to serve the Coahuiltecan Indians. At its peak, the mission had some 250–300 Indians living there.

The simple beauty of the Concepción chapel is shown in the intricate carved stonework on the church entrance.

The stone church, finished in 1755 and made out of a limestone called tufa from a nearby quarry, was located in the southeastern portion of the walled-in square. These walls had Indian living quarters built into them, and these along with the granary, which extended southward from the present-day sacristy, no longer exist. Besides a convento attached to the church, there were also carpenter, blacksmith, and textile shops. An irrigation ditch, or acequia, flowed through the compound farther west of the church. Outside the enclosure was the mission farm where crops such as corn, beans, watermelons, and sweet potatoes were grown. Still farther away was the mission ranch, which had its own brand.

In 1794, Concepción was partially secularized, and some of its land distributed to the Indians. For a while it was a sub-mission of San José; then it was completely closed down in 1813.

About this time, a revolutionary army led by Mexican Bernardo Gutierrez headquartered here while it attacked local Spanish officials in an earlier aborted attempt to get Texas out from under Spanish rule.

Later on in October of 1835 was the so-called Battle of Concepción, which came about when a volunteer army of Texans headed by Stephen F. Austin marched from Gonzales to capture San Antonio at the beginning of the Texas Revolution. There were several skirmishes in the area as the army waited on the fringe of town—one of them a quarter of a mile from Concepción led by Jim Bowie, James Fannin, and Juan Seguin. Eventually old Ben Milam took the forces into San Antonio and handily defeated General Cos. This defeat in turn led to General Santa Anna's return grudge fight at the Alamo.

In the 1840s Concepción was used by the U.S. Army as a military camp, and John R. Bartlett, who visited the mission in 1850, described still another use: "The two towers and dome . . . make quite an imposing appearance when seen from a distance, but on approaching it, we found it not only desolated but desecrated, the church portion being used as an enclosure for cattle, the filth from which covered the floor . . . a foot or more."

Fortunately, along came the Brothers of Mary, founders of St. Mary's School (now a local university), who occupied and restored the place from around 1859 to 1911. They restored the church and used the farm land to supply the school. And in the hot summer, faculty members even used it as a vacation spot for swimming and fishing. In more recent times, St. John's Seminary was built next door and a Catholic orphanage was established across Mission Road.

ARCHITECTURE AND RESTORATION

Concepción's church originally had colorful flower-like geometric designs painted on its facade, though this effect is difficult to imagine now with the plain greyish-white stone that predominates the chapel. About the only remnants left of these frescoes can be seen inside in the confessional/belfry, baptistry, and convento.

The church, made of tufa, has twin towers and a Moorish dome. The tops of the towers are pyramidal with four lookout windows and a tiny iron cross on each. The entrance is the only really decorative part of Concepción's architecture. Sculptured stonework frames large wooden doors. The design features a triangle above with a cross and shell-shaped recess in it. To the sides are half columns and flowered geometric designs.

Inside, the church is laid out in cruciform (cross-shaped) style with a vaulted ceiling. White walls are set off with accent colors of teal, mustard, and maroon, and Spanish-type candle fixtures. At the rear is the usual

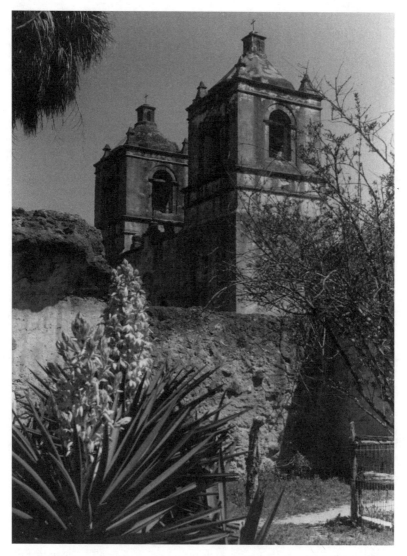

The twin bell towers of Concepción church give this mission its distinctive look.

transept and altar. The floor is flagstone, and the walls are four feet thick. The outside and inside facings of the walls are of cut stones, with the space in between filled with small stones and adobe.

To the left as you come in is the confessional room, or belfry (or St. Michael's Chapel). To the right is the baptistry. The baptismal font is of sculptured stone and used to be lined with copper. You'll see some of those unusual frescoes mentioned earlier in both of these rooms. In the baptistery above the baptismal font, a faint wall fresco of Christ on the

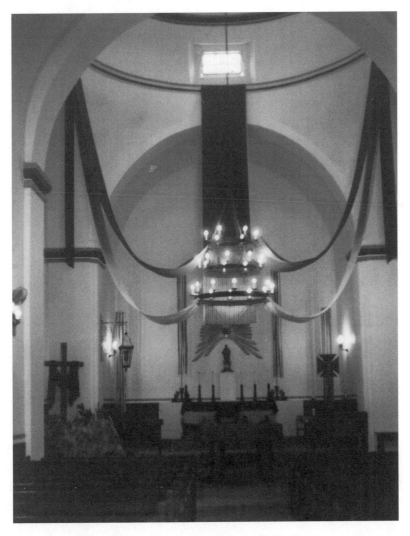

The domed Concepción church is well known for its acoustics.

cross can be seen. In the other room on the left is a fresco design on the ceiling. To the right rear of the sanctuary is the sacristy, or room for the priests' vestments, etc. Above it is what they call the "Father President's office," once used as a missionary administrative office. A small window looks down from it into the sanctuary.

A display info panel explains: "In this office Fr. Francisco Cayetana del Aponte y Lis attended to the work of administering the Queretaran missions of San Antonio and Texas. Fr. Francisco lived at Concepción from 1748–1757. He participated in the building of the stone church. The president of the missions, or Father President, presided over the missions and communicated with the Commissary Prefect of Missions. Two apostolic colleges in New Spain, Santa Cruz de Queretaro and Nuestra Señora de Guadalupe de Zacetecas, established missions in Texas and supplied them with well-trained missionaries." Be careful on the steep steps going up to this second-story room, and particularly when coming down. Father President definitely had to be in good shape.

Frescoes

Now here's more about those unusual interior paintings, or frescoes. The more restored ones are located in the convento, which is attached to

Mission Concepción

1 Church
2 Sacristy
3 Father President's Office
4 Convenio and *Corredor*
5 Well
6 Grotto
7 Quarry

the church's front south tower. The convento consists of several rooms, connected with a walkway. In the library room, you'll find the most fascinating of the frescoes. On the ceiling is the rather humorous painting of a round sun face with eyes and a mustache. For years, before the frescoes were restored by experts using the same techniques used to clean the Sistine Chapel, only one eye could be seen, and it came to be popularly called "God's Eye"—as though God was peering down at you from the ceiling. Then it was cleaned to expose the whole face with a sunburst around it. So now, it's not always referred to as "God's Eye" anymore. The park staff think maybe it was a Spanish medallion or the king of Spain at the time of the missions. In the same room can be seen remnants of other frescoes, including a cross with Spanish helmets on it.

The convento has a roofed corridor that runs the length of the front with arched openings looking out on the patio and well.

As said before, comparatively little restoration has been done here at Concepción. What has fallen into disarray has been left there, and what has lasted has been left alone. Of course, some minor restoration was done in the latter half of the 1800s by the Brothers of Mary and the Catholic Church to clean it up from the cattle pen era. But all of this is what makes up the allure of Concepción. Even left as it was, it still has a classic grace, and you know this is where and how missionaries actually led their lives and worshipped centuries ago.

DIRECTIONS TO CONCEPCIÓN

If you're downtown in San Antonio, begin at the intersection of Market and South Alamo Street (the Alamo and HemisFair Park front this street). Go south on South Alamo, then turn left on St. Mary's, and just follow the Mission Trail signs. St. Mary's turns into Roosevelt, and after going under the underpass, turn right on Lone Star, and then go straight ahead on Mission Road. Stay on it about a half mile until you reach the corner of Felisa and Mission Road, where Concepción's parking lot is located.

If you are coming from somewhere else in the city, get on the Hwy 90 freeway, also IH 10, and exit at Probandt; go south a couple of blocks and turn left on Mitchell. Then turn right on Mission Road. Concepción is only two blocks down, where the road intersects Felisa.

Maybe you don't want to drive yourself. Ask about the regular city bus (VIA) schedule that runs strictly between downtown and the missions, with reasonable fares and frequent stops at the missions so that you can get on and off when you want.

TOURING CONCEPCIÓN

The park service offers informal guided tours during the day. Several commercial bus tours stop at Concepción on their mission tours, which embark from near the Alamo daily.

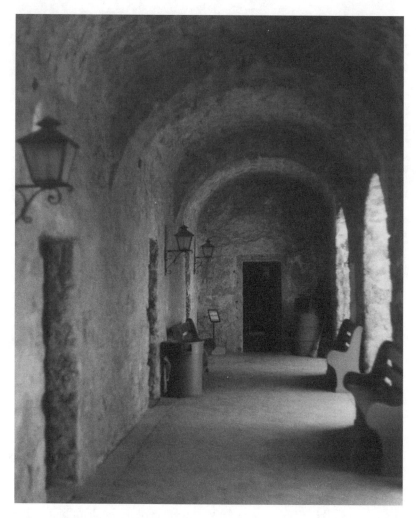

The arched corridor on the convento building is pictured here.

HISTORICAL DISPLAYS AND PARK STAFF BUILDING

While at this time there are no exhibits at Concepción, the National Park Service has placed in different areas pleasing informational panels, including ones on the Spanish missionary empire, Franciscan friars, Coahuiltecan Indians, mission architecture, and mission life. There is also a short, unadorned slide show about mission history in one of the convento rooms. Just punch the button on the slide machine and activate it yourself.

The small park staff building is near the parking lot as you drive up. Here you can find out when the next informal tour will take place, buy books on the missions, and generally get information. Benches, a drinking fountain, and restrooms are also here.

ANNUAL EVENTS

December 8

Feast of Immaculate Conception—Mass service. Open to the public.

OTHER SIGHTS NEARBY

If you don't intend to follow the Mission Trail south to tour the other three missions, then you might like to take in another historic site, the Yturri-Edmunds Home and Mill, at 257 Yellowstone (534-8237). The mid-1800s adobe structure and grist mill is only about one-half mile north on Mission Road, where Yellowstone intersects. The San Antonio Conservation Society runs the home and offers guided tours and demonstrations. There is a fee. Days and hours open may vary by season.

MISSION SAN JUAN

Mission San Juan Capistrano

**9100 block of Graf, at Ashley Road, San Antonio • Small museum
Open daily 9 a.m. to 5 p.m.; closed Thanksgiving, Christmas Day and
New Year's Day • Free • (210) 534-0749**

Historians are wont to disagree among themselves, but many think Mission San Juan is near the site on the San Antonio River where Spaniards first discovered and named the area in 1691.

"We found at this place the rancheria of the Indians of the Payaya tribe . . . I called this place San Antonio de Padua, because it was his feast day. In the language of the Indians, it is called Yanaguana . . . On this day, there were so many buffaloes that the horses stampeded . . .," wrote Fr. Damian Massanet, whose cohort on the expedition, Governor Don Domingo de Teran, also claims to have named the area.

Whoever takes the credit, the name for San Antonio, or Saint Anthony, stuck. Teran got the idea to put missions here.

"I discovered that they (the Indians) were docile and affectionate, were naturally friendly, and were decidedly agreeable to us. I saw the possibility of using them to form missions, the first on the Rio Grande, at the presidio, and another at this point," he wrote in his diary. Later friars would have the same idea. Thus San Antonio became a way station for the missions farther away in East Texas and eventually the capital of the Texas provincial territory.

Unlike Concepción, San Juan still has its square, and it appears straight out of the eighteenth century, with its bucolic setting in an old, rather isolated part of town. It is third on the Mission Trail in south San Antonio, and quite endearing. Again, this is part of the San Antonio Missions National Historical Park.

This pastoral setting will greet you at San Juan.

The charm of San Juan lies not in any stately architecture but in its simplicity. It is in fact a very plain mission. The church is even stark, with only the bell tower wall to give it any religious character. But because it is surrounded by trees and foliage and few houses in this sparsely settled area, the quaint aura of the eighteenth century is inescapable when you enter the square from the arched southwest entrance. The courtyard within the square (which actually isn't a square but an odd-shaped rectangle) is lined with green grass and clover. The church (still in use), convento, and ruins of the hospederia (guest room) and Indian quarters help form the walls of the mission compound.

San Juan (short for Mission San Juan Capistrano) is one of the three missions, along with Concepción and Espada, which relocated to San Antonio from East Texas in 1731.

After first obtaining a map at the park entrance, simply follow the plaques around the square. You can easily view it in 30 minutes, but I suggest you tarry longer at the restored convento-museum. It is a fine little mission museum and has some excellent exhibits about archeological finds and the Coahuiltecan Indians. Currently open to the public are the church, convento museum, and a post-colonial house. The rest are remnants of walls or off-limits restored residences used by church or park officials.

The grassy areas outside the square are fine for picnicking, and parks are only blocks away. No fast food franchises are close by. But then if there were, the rustic appeal of the place would vanish.

HISTORY

San Juan not only started out in another place, East Texas, it started out with another name: San José de los Nazonis. But since there was already a mission by the name of San José when it moved to San Antonio in 1731, the title was changed. Mission San Juan Capistrano means mission of St. John Capistran. St. John was a roving Franciscan preacher who became famous for leading a Christian army in a victory against the Turks in 1456.

The mission first started out in 1716 near present Cushing, not far from Nacogdoches. Meant to serve the Nazoni Indians, it was soon abandoned by Spain in 1719 when the French became hostile. Spain returned in 1721 to reestablish it, but soon, cost cutting caused the nearby presidio to close down. The three missions (Concepción and Espada were the other two), without any military protection, requested to be moved elsewhere. First they tried a spot on the Colorado River in 1730, but this didn't work out either. Soon they all ended up in San Antonio, bag and baggage hauled tediously by cart from East Texas.

The mission began with only crude mud huts on its present spot on the east bank of the San Antonio River, south of Mission San José and about seven miles from downtown San Antonio. But by about 1745, modest stone buildings had been erected for a friary and a granary. And by 1756, a church, whose foundations can still be seen on the south side near the present restrooms, was built. Some 265 Indians lived in the compound around this time. The remnants of the square today reflect its appearance in the 1780s, with Indian quarters on the north and west walls.

Two missionaries, along with several Spanish soldiers with swivel guns to ward off the Apaches, minded the store. The standard mission carpenter, blacksmith, and textile shops flourished, and crops of corn, melons, beans, chiles, and cotton sprouted in the nearby farm fields. San Juan's ranch, Rancho Pataguilla, was some miles southeast of it and provided meat and wool. Once a week, cattle were driven from there, slaughtered, and given to the Indians.

Sometime in the 1760s when the Indian population was high and the mission thriving, a newer and larger church was begun on the east side of the square. It was never finished, and the ruins can still be seen today. San Juan was partially secularized, along with the other missions, in 1794. It became a sort of sub-mission, overseen by the Espada missionary. The present church was probably built originally as a granary in the 1770s.

In 1824 San Juan was completely demissionized, although Spanish and Indian families continued to live in the area. The old stone and adobe house on the edge of the east wall is from this post-colonial period.

Though San Juan deteriorated over the years, it doesn't seem to have been subject to the destruction the other missions experienced. They were used as cattle pens and stomping grounds for rambunctious soldiers. San Juan continued to be an active, viable community. The church's roof fell in but was repaired in 1909, and since then it has been regularly used as a parish church.

Mission San Juan

1 Church and Sacristy
2 Late Colonial Church Ruins
3 Early Colonial Church Ruins
4 Convento
5 *Hospederia*
6 Ruins of Convento Workrooms
7 Well
8 *Porteria*
9 North Wall Indian Quarters

10 West Wall Indian Quarters
11 Compound Walls
     and Wall Ruins
12 Meeting and Storage Room
13 Office and Rectory
14 Post-Colonial House
     Ruins Converted
     to Restrooms
15 Post-Colonial House

ARCHITECTURE AND RESTORATION

As mentioned, San Juan's church is outwardly unadorned but still has a certain primitive grace to it. Even the visiting Fr. Morfi remarked of San Juan in 1777, "The church is neat and in good order, though it does not compare with those described [Alamo, Concepción, and San José]." Though his comment probably referred to an earlier church here, it shows that San Juan was much less grand than the other missions.

The wood door entrance of the rectangular stone church appears to be an afterthought, it is so small compared to other churches—probably because this building wasn't initially intended to be a church, but maybe, as mentioned, a granary. The one identifying characteristic is the Spanish bell tower at the end, which makes for an interesting silhouette against the sky with its three bells and tiny iron cross at the top. Surprisingly, the lack of rococo on the church and the quaintness of the buildings in the square make the mission an excellent unspoiled photo subject.

Inside the church is just as modest. It simply doesn't have the magnitude of some mission chapels. There is no domed ceiling—just a flat one with beams. The room is a rectangle, narrower than it is tall, and the walls are painted white, with a colorful Indian-like design border accenting them. Simple wooden pews and altar (though there are a gilded backdrop and religious statues) indicate that this is not an affluent parish. But the pews are freshly varnished and the reddish tile floor is polished. Plus it has the comfort of air-conditioning, not always found at the mission chapels. It's really an inviting place to worship.

These gabled buildings on the edge of the mission square are actually reproductions, but they fit into the centuries-aged ambiance.

Apparently at one time, crude, colorful frescoes lined the inside walls, depicting musicians playing instruments. When asked about them in the late 1880s, local priest Father Bouchu explained, "They were probably permitted to satisfy the Indian nature's love of color."

Around 1967, restoration began on the church and convento. Two old-looking houses with gabled roofs were built atop the foundation ruins of the Indian homes and nineteenth-century dwellings on the northern part of the west wall. To the novice they look old, except for the shingle roofs.

MUSEUM AND ARCHEOLOGY

History got buried literally at San Juan. During restoration work begun in 1967, archeological excavations uncovered some graves in both foundations of the churches, plus innumerable artifacts in other areas. A short slide show and explanations of what was found can be seen in the small museum in the restored convento next to the mission entrance. The artifacts themselves, such as arrowheads, bone tools, pottery shards, and coins are also attractively displayed.

The skeletons (not on display) from the east church ruins date from the 1760s to 1790s, and archeologists were thus able to make some observations about the Coahuiltecan Indians: "The average male was 5.7 feet tall, and the average female 5.4 feet . . . The pathology study of their bones revealed the diseases they suffered: arthritis, osteoporosis, osteitis, paget's

The starkly simple San Juan church has only one religious characteristic, its triangular-shaped three-bell tower. No wonder—it started out as a granary.

disease, and syphilis." The Indians seemed to be plagued with some of the same diseases that still plague us. Excavations also turned up the fact that underneath the present church was an old foundation that probably served as an earlier granary.

This is a small museum, but the exhibits are well done for mission history enthusiasts, and the kids will enjoy the Indian artifacts. Besides the Coahuiltecan displays, others include data on the building of San Juan, the establishment of San Antonio missions, presidios, the economy of the missions, ranching, secularization, and the Franciscans.

DIRECTIONS TO SAN JUAN

If coming from downtown to see this mission only, take IH 37 south, then exit on S.E. Military Drive going west. Take a left on South Presa, going south, and later a right on Graf which will take you a few blocks to the mission. You can see the bell tower; just follow the signs to the parking lot and entrance.

However, if you've been on the Mission Trail visiting the other missions, you have just been to San José. As you come out of the San José parking lot, turn left on Mission Road, and just follow the Mission Trail signs by way of Mission Parkway to San Juan. In other words, San Juan is farther south of San José.

Picnicking Along the Mission Parkway

Between San José and San Juan there is a particularly nice green country-like area on the Mission Parkway, a roadway that follows the San Antonio River. Some picnic tables dot the parkway. Stop for lunch or a snack between missions. Two things to be forewarned of: This is an isolated area and not a good place to stop alone, and it's also affected by heavy rains, with the river rising over low-water crossings.

SAN JUAN WOODLANDS HIKING TRAIL

To the back of San Juan is a hiking trail about one third of a mile long. Although it is asphalt paved, it is not for bikes. It only takes about fifteen minutes to walk it, and it loops along the San Antonio River. Beware, don't go off the path into the woods. Mean old fire ants and poison ivy lurk there. You may purchase a small booklet about the trail for a tiny fee in the mission park office.

TOURING SAN JUAN

The National Park Service usually gives guided tours to individuals, or you can pick up a map at the entrance and proceed around the square by yourself.

Local commercial bus companies do give tours of the missions.

MISSION ESPADA

Mission San Francisco de la Espada

10040 Espada Road, San Antonio • Open daily 9 a.m. to 5 p.m.; closed
Thanksgiving, Christmas Day and New Year's Day • Free
(210) 627-2021

Much like a lonely stepchild, Mission Espada languishes on the southern
fringe of San Antonio as the farthest away of the city's missions. The setting looms pastoral, because it *is.* Farmland and a few small houses sur-
round the mission much like they did centuries ago, despite the fact that
the mission lies just south of busy Loop 410.

Espada is a homely mission, but therein lies its simple charm. Much of it
is in foundation ruins and unrestored, except for the convento and the
endearing rustic chapel with its bell tower. Interestingly enough, Mission
San Francisco de la Espada has a longer history than the other San Antonio
missions, because it was the original San Francisco de los Tejas, the first
mission established in East Texas by the Spanish in 1690. It was abandoned
and moved to several locations because of French threats and hostile Indians before it ended up in San Antonio in 1731 with a slight name change.

Strangely, while part of the mission itself fell into ruins, Espada's irrigation system still stands today, miraculously watering the same land it did
hundreds of years ago. In fact, it's probably the oldest acequia system still
working in the United States, with the only Spanish aqueduct left standing. The aqueduct, which can be seen on the way to or from Espada, inge-
niously carries water from the dam on the San Antonio River across
Piedras Creek to the mission and the lands below.

If you're taking in all of the missions on the Mission Trail, it's probably
best to see the aqueduct on the way from San Juan to Espada. Aqueduct
Park is located just off Espada Road, and roughly one and a half miles farther south is Espada Mission itself.

There isn't a great deal to see at Espada in terms of touring the structures,
because only the chapel and information center are actually open to the
public. You can still view the foundation ruins and get the lay of the compound. These compound walls are shaped in a slightly irregular square.

You can park on the south side of the mission and enter through an opening in the south wall. To the right in the southeast corner is the information
center. Stop here to ask for a free mission map or to see the short slide show,
and glance at whatever brief exhibits (such as a weaving loom) happen to be
current. On that same corner is an object worth studying, the corner bastion. Similar to the restored one at San José, this is the only surviving bastion left intact in the local missions. A squat, round rock fortification, it contains holes for cannons and muskets to defend the adjacent walls.

Out here at Espada you can feel what it was like to be isolated in a
remote mission. Being the farthest away, it was particularly preyed on by
the Apache Indians. Though the compound itself was defensible, Apaches
would steal horses and swoop down on individuals straying from the complex. One day in the 1730s five mission Indian women and two boys went

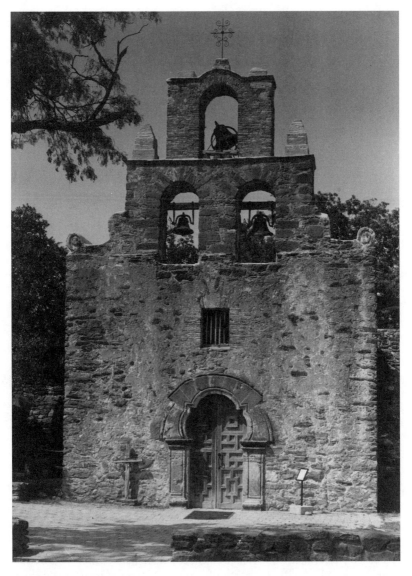

The Moorish arch framing the doors is the only decorative stonework at the quaint, diminutive chapel at Espada, which also boasts a three-bell wall tower.

out to gather fruit. The boys ended up captured and the hapless women murdered.

Likewise, you can imagine Mission Espada as a likely camp for the Texan army during the Texas Revolution. In October 1835, James Bowie and James Fannin and their troops spent a few days here and fought off a band of Mexican soldiers.

Make the rounds of the square with map in hand to see the outline of the various foundation ruins, including the granary, the unfinished church, and the Indian quarters. The convento has been restored, but is closed to the public. Espada, like the other San Antonio missions, is a thriving parish church. The chapel itself is certainly nothing grand like San José's or Concepción's, but nevertheless it is appealing in its simplicity and warm intimacy.

Before leaving Espada, the stouthearted might walk the few rustic trails wandering outside the walls toward the river. But it's very isolated out here. Don't expect any fast-food shops nearby. There is peace and tranquility here, disturbed only by an occasional hum of a single-engine plane from a nearby small airfield.

THE ESPADA AQUEDUCT AND SAN ANTONIO'S UNIQUE EARLY WATER SYSTEM

Watering crops wasn't so easy in mission times when you consider there was no modern irrigation, much less a water system. That's why the Spanish shrewdly built the missions near the San Antonio River. There was still the problem of getting water from the river to the fields, and thus a unique acequia (canal or ditch) system was created along the river for the various mission farms. Today you can still view remnants of this open canal system in parts of the city, which continued to use it up until the 1870s. The Espada Aqueduct remains in use as a salute to the Spanish friars' ingenuity.

The crude beginnings of this unusual water system started first around 1719 with the Acequia Madre, or "Mother Ditch" (the Alamo Ditch), designed to irrigate fields for Mission San Antonio de Valero.

The Acequia San José is thought to have been completed around 1730, and the Concepción, San Juan, and Espada canals begun around 1731. Then finally a canal system (Acequia San Pedro) that brought water from San Pedro Springs was started for the townfolk and presidio in 1738.

The Espada acequia system posed more problems than the others. Water had to be brought from the Espada dam about two miles north on the San Antonio River *across* Piedras Creek. For this reason the arched stone aqueduct was built to carry water across the creek bed to the Espada fields below. The aged, vine-covered structure still sends water down the trough today to water the land near Espada.

You can scrutinize the aqueduct in Aqueduct Park, which is approximately one and a half miles north of Espada Mission by road. It is just off Espada Road. There is a small, clean area for picnicking right by the aqueduct as it passes over the tiny Piedras Creek. And there are plenty of rustic hiking trails on the hill above the aqueduct that are guaranteed to burn up kiddie energy. But remember that this is a somewhat isolated area, and be on the lookout for your safety.

The Espada dam and canal system are thought to have been started around 1731, but the aqueduct itself was not completed until around 1740. The 270-foot dam is another unusual engineering feat. After hundreds of years it still stands, with the layers of brush, gravel, and rocks cemented together over time by the lime salts in the water. For years people thought

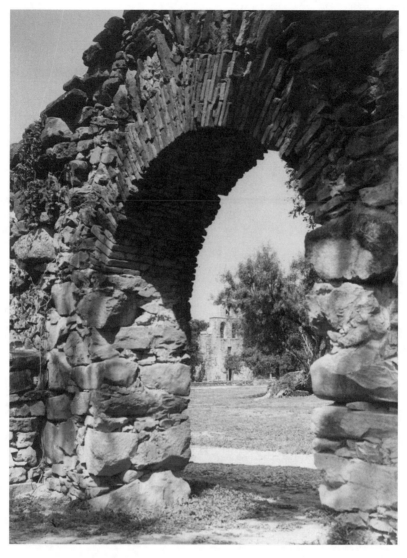

One of the few walls remaining of Espada's square frames the chapel.

the dam curved the wrong way, but that is because only one corner of a box dam shows. The other corner is under the surface. National Park Service researchers discovered that the San Juan dam was also still standing. It was hidden in a dry bed of the river cut off by rechanneling.

The Espada Ditch Company did some patch-repair work on the system in 1895. In 1941, the San Antonio Conservation Society bought up land adjacent to the aqueduct, and the aqueduct was declared a national historic landmark in 1965.

Probably the oldest acequia system in the nation can be found in San Antonio. The ancient Espada Aqueduct at nearby Aqueduct Park is still transporting water to land below.

HISTORY

Keeping up with Espada's elusive history is like following a soap opera heroine who keeps remarrying and changing her name. As said earlier, the mission was first established as San Francisco de los Tejas in East Texas in 1690 when the Spanish wanted to stake out their claim in Texas. They disliked France encroaching on their territory. When the ill-fated La Salle had wandered across Texas, Spain stepped up its mission activity. An expedition of Alonso de Leon and Fr. Damian Massanet founded a mission on San Pedro Creek near present-day Weches to ostensibly serve the area's Indians, whom they called the Tejas.

Epidemics and hostile Indians led the missionaries to abandon San Francisco three years later. The friars actually burned it down themselves. A log mission replica is now located in the vicinity of this former site at Mission Tejas State Historical Park (see later section for more details).

It wasn't until some years later in 1716 that Spain decided to reoccupy East Texas and start up even more missions. One of the six begun was the reincarnation of San Francisco at a site ten miles farther east of its first location. The new site was on the Neches River, near present-day Alto. This time the mission was called Nuestro Padre San Francisco de los Tejas, and the missionary life was still tough sledding.

The French drove the Spanish missionaries out in another three years, and the mission had to be reestablished again in 1721, apparently at the

Mission Espada

1 Church and Sacristy
2 Walls of Granary
   and Late Colonial
   Church
3 Convento Converted to
   Rectory and Office
4 Convento Well
5 Workshop Walls
6 Walls of the Late Colonial Granary
7 Indian Qaurters, South Wall of Compound
8 Indian Quarters, East Wall of Compound
9 Northeast Wall
10 Indian Quarters, North Wall of Compound

11 Indian Quarters, West Wall of Compound
12 Chavagneux House Ruins
13 Bastion and Adjoining Rooms,
   now Visitor Center)
14 Old Schoolhouse
15 Oaks House and Convent Ruins
16 Conti House Ruins
17 Cuellar House Ruins
18 Old Classroom
19 Walls Associated with Gateway
20 Camposanto
21 Sluice Gate
22 Kilns
24 Well Northwest of Compound

same site. This time it was called San Francisco de los Neches (supposedly for the Neche Indians). Spanish economizing closed down the nearby protective presidio and sent San Francisco and two other missions (Concepción and San Juan, then called San José de los Nazonis) packing once again. After locating briefly on a Colorado River site in Central Texas, all the missions finally landed in 1731 at San Antonio where San Francisco was renamed for the last time as Mission San Francisco de la Espada. This means mission of St. Francis of La Espada. *Espada* is the word for sword, but no one seems to know why this word is in the name, unless it honored some prominent person's name. Whatever, the mission has come to be known simply as "Espada."

A stone sacristy was finished in the 1740s, and this is what is now still used as the small church. Even before that, sometime around 1740, Espada's famous aqueduct was completed. A granary was built around 1762 near the south square wall, and it was later used as a church. But the quality control proved poor, and eventually the completed building had to be torn down. Indian quarters were located in the square walls. Espada's ranch, Rancho de las Cabras, was located some miles away on the San Antonio River near Floresville.

The peak Indian population was probably around 200. A Father Garcia, stationed here in 1760, wrote a guide on the Coahuiltecan language used by the various Indian tribes and included a few interesting observations of their habits, such as their penchant for eating the narcotic buds of the cactus peyotl and making liquor from the mountain-laurel bean.

Espada was partially secularized in 1794 and completely so in 1824. In the 1820s, Mexican troops were occasionally stationed here to protect settlers, and in 1835, as mentioned earlier, Texas revolutionaries camped and fought here.

The place fell mostly into ruins after this, until along came a guardian angel in the form of Father Francis Bouchu. Bouchu both lived and worked here and almost single-handedly rebuilt the original little chapel himself. He first came to San Antonio as assistant pastor at San Fernando Church, but fell in love with the old Espada mission and ministered to the parishioners there from 1858 to 1907. A jack-of-all-trades, he also cranked out on his own little printing press a Spanish language catechism, which came to be used in several dioceses. Ever since Bouchu's era, Espada has served as a parish church, and for a while it served as a parochial school.

ARCHITECTURE AND RESTORATION

The dominant feature of this mission is naturally the little stone chapel built around 1745. It is by no means a grandiose structure but simply a rudimentary pastoral church, with its only significant feature being the appealing three-bell tower on the front wall.

The only bit of slight embellishment on the entire building is at the entrance where a sculptured stone Moorish arch frames the carved wooden doors. Actually, this small chapel was initially intended to be just the sacristy of a much larger church that never got built.

On the left of the church's front is a crude, wooden cross, which has a long tale behind it. Local legend says that about 1870 the congregation carried a wooden cross about the compound praying for rain, and lo and behold, torrents fell. So Father Bouchu placed it there to remind them of the power of prayer. The current small cross is obviously of more recent vintage.

Inside, the small chapel is shaped in a cross, with a red tile floor and a flat ceiling of rough-hewn beams. White walls and wooden pews face a simple altar with fresh flowers, lighted candles, and three carved wooden statues. One is thought to be of St. Francis and original with the church. The other two are of Mary and Jesus.

Don't overlook the well to the left of the chapel and in front of the arched convento. It has wrought iron grillwork on the top similar to the one at Concepción.

As for Espada restoration, it began during Father Bouchu's tenure of 1858–1907 and his one-man job of dedicated renovation. When he arrived, only the rear wall and facade of the chapel were standing. He rebuilt the side walls on old foundations and added a roof. Author William Corner, who wrote of the padre in 1890, called him a "priest, lawyer, bricklayer, stone mason, photographer, historian, printer . . . He is simple, unaffected, and garrulous, and meets the wants of the little settlement."

Further restoration has been done since 1909 in piecemeal fashion by the Catholic Church and the National Park Service.

DIRECTIONS TO ESPADA

If you come from downtown to see only Mission Espada (and don't take the Mission Trail tour of all four), take IH 37 south. Espada is on the southern edge of San Antonio. Turn right or west onto Loop 410 and drive for almost four miles until you exit at Roosevelt Avenue, where you turn left under the freeway, make a U-turn, and go eastward on the freeway access road for about two miles until you turn right at the Espada exit. This puts you onto Espada Road, where you are headed southeast towards the mission. When you sight Espada, don't turn on the first road into it. Wait and turn left onto Camino Coahuilteca Street. The parking lot will be on your left, and you enter the mission park at a gate in the south square wall. The information center is at the southeast corner of the mission compound.

If you tour all four missions on the Mission Trail, you will be coming from Mission San Juan. There are two routes from San Juan. You can go to the right from San Juan onto Villa Main, going south under Loop 410 and then right, or west onto Camino Coahuilteca, which will take you to the mission's doorstep. But because there is a low water crossing on this route, the National Park Service sometimes recommends taking a left on Ashley Road (going west). There will be signs directing you where to turn off of Ashley onto Espada Road, which takes you to Mission Espada, approximately two miles farther south. On this route you can stop by Espada Aqueduct at Aqueduct Park, which is just off Espada Road, on the way to

An original fortified corner bastion still survives in the wall ruins of Espada's square.

the mission. However, the route leading from San Juan to Espada, particularly by way of the Espada Aqueduct, can be very confusing. Ask a park ranger for directions before driving there.

TOURING ESPADA

Usually limited staff precludes giving informal tours, but there's not that much to see here anyway. Just get a map from the visitor center, and follow it.

Commercial bus tours of the missions leave daily from near the Alamo in downtown San Antonio.

GOLIAD MISSION AND PRESIDIO

Goliad is a pleasurable surprise in the litany of small Texas towns. It's chock-full of historic battlegrounds and grave sites and even has a bona fide "hanging tree." It is Texas history in the flesh, right up there alongside San Antonio and San Jacinto. So you might as well take a detour from San Antonio down to Goliad, only about 95 miles to the southeast, to relive the Texas revolutionary saga.

Investigate Mission Espíritu and Presidio La Bahía, the site of the Goliad Massacre, where Colonel James Fannin and about 341 of his men were executed by the Mexicans only a few weeks after the disastrous fall of the Alamo. This is the next chapter in the story of Texas independence, which fostered another battle cry shouted at San Jacinto—"Remember Goliad."

Goliad embraces a rare combination of a restored mission and presidio, all in one vicinity, as they were traditionally set up by the Spanish in the

1700s. That's why the presidio, or fort, is included in this book. The mission was designed to proselytize the native Indians and the presidio to fend off those who didn't want to be proselytized and other hostile forces, like the French.

This is the only really complete and intact mission-presidio duo we know of in Texas. For instance, the presidio in San Antonio is long gone, and only the chapel of San Elizario Presidio remains in El Paso.

PICNICKING/CAMPING AT GOLIAD STATE HISTORICAL PARK

Both Mission Espíritu Santo and La Bahía Presidio are located just south of Goliad on Hwy 183. And conveniently, Espíritu Santo is actually part of Goliad State Historical Park, which has excellent, clean facilities for camping and picnicking. Besides screen shelters and RV hookups, there is a pool and fishing on the San Antonio River. See a fifteen-minute film and exhibit on Texas missions at the park headquarters.

SPECIAL EVENTS AT MISSION AND PRESIDIO

Look for some colorful special events during the year at both the mission and the presidio, particularly during December and Christmastime. The town itself has "Christmas in Goliad," and both mission and presidio usually join in with coinciding events, all of which happen around an early weekend in December. For instance, Mission Espíritu will be decorated with Christmas lights and may have a choir perform "The Messiah," while Presidio La Bahía may have its living history encampment, Texas Frontier Rendezvous, inside the fort grounds where frontier lifestyles are portrayed.

At other times of the year, look for more living history enactments at the fort, such as the Battle of the White Cow/Siege around February and then, around March 27, the anniversary observance of the Goliad massacre. Mission Espíritu usually has a spring choir concert around April.

OTHER SIGHTS IN GOLIAD

Goliad is resplendent with historical markers. The General Ignacio Zaragoza birthplace is just outside La Bahía's walls, and the Fannin Memorial, where the massacred troops were buried, is just one-quarter mile away. The site of the Battle of Coleto Creek, or Fannin Battleground State Historic Site, is nine miles east of Goliad on Hwy 59, but there's not much to actually see there. Downtown Goliad, or the courthouse square, however, shouldn't be missed. This is the kind of place to mosey and enjoy small-town America without urban traffic hassles. Park on the square with its 1894 courthouse complete with hanging tree, and shop and eat.

Incidentally, there was another mission, Rosario, built in the Goliad area in 1754. But only ruins are left and they were covered with brush and closed to the public as of this writing; so I don't recommend taking time to see the site unless you're a die-hard historian. The ruins are located about six miles west of Goliad on Hwy 59 (see **Other Mission Sites and Ruins Around the State**).

WHERE TO GET INFORMATION

Goliad County Chamber of Commerce

P.O. Box 606
Goliad, Texas 77963
(361) 645-3563 or (800) 848-8674

Goliad State Historical Park

108 Park Road 6
Goliad, Texas 77963
(361) 645-3405

Presidio La Bahía

P.O. Box 57
Goliad, Texas 77963
(361) 645-3752

MISSION ESPÍRITU SANTO

Mission Espíritu Santo de Zuñiga

On Hwy 183, about one-quarter mile south of Goliad in Goliad State Historical Park • Museum, camping, and recreational facilities • Open 8 a.m. to 5 p.m. daily except Christmas • Park entrance fee ($2 adults) serves as admission • (361) 645-3405 • W

Mission Espíritu Santo has a lot going for it that makes it novel among Texas missions. To begin with, it's situated in the middle of a state park with recreational and camping facilities so that you can combine a camp-out with a tour of a historical mission. In fact, the very reason for Goliad State Historical Park's existence is the mission.

Espíritu Santo has been handsomely restored and a museum has been added. There are weekly weaving and spinning demonstrations, plus a small petting zoo and a nature trail that shows how the Aranama Indians utilized native plants for survival. In all, the activities are varied enough to keep the whole family sufficiently entertained.

Another unusual aspect about Espíritu Santo is the importance it played in Texas' ultimate industry, cattle. Many of the missions had cattle ranches all their own, because the Spaniards were seasoned cattlemen and brought the herds along with them. But Espíritu had the largest ranch of all. It stretched roughly between Goliad and San Antonio and had an estimated 40,000 head!

High on a hill near Goliad sits the magnificent restored church of Espíritu Santo.

Like the presidio down the road, the mission started out on the Texas coast at the site of La Salle's defunct colony. (The presidio was founded in 1721, the mission in 1722.) The two, which became known as the La Bahía mission and presidio, moved again in tandem and ended up in 1749 on the San Antonio River at what is now Goliad. Here the mission ministered mainly to the Aranama Indians, who proved more amenable to mission life than had the Karankawas.

To get to Espíritu, stop at the park headquarters and pay. The mission is just behind the headquarters and up a grassy hill. The whole park is neatly kept, the mission in particular. It's an inspiring sight to view Espíritu's romantic colonial structure standing out in the rural countryside.

The park staff will give you a park brochure, which has a more detailed map of the mission on the back. From there stroll up the walk to Espíritu. Head first for the museum, which is just left of the church entrance and in the old granary. Here attendants will be glad to answer questions for your guided tour. During the week in the school year, attendance is slow. But in summertime and on weekends it picks up.

What is there to see? Begin with the church. Its elegant facade is well proportioned and very pleasing to the eye. Sculptured stonework encloses the wooden door entrance and to the right is a covered octangular bell tower with a cross on top. A few Moorish points—or teeth—stick up at the rear roof edge, much like they do at Mission Concepción in San Antonio. Inside, the church has towering white walls with a bright red border, back-dropped by a colorful red and gold accentuated altar and baptismal room to the side. There are no pews because this is not used as a parish church.

The church, the granary (where the museum is) and mission school workshop behind them are the limits of what can be physically toured inside. The rest of the mission grounds are simply low ruin walls or foundations that can be quickly viewed by glancing and walking around the square compound. However, the small petting zoo pen for big and little kids is located in the northwest corner of the compound.

PARK RECREATION FACILITIES AND NATURE TRAIL

If you still feel like more walking, take the nature trail that starts just outside the northwest corner of the mission square. Called the Aranama Trail, it's only about one third of a mile long. But first be sure to get that free brochure explaining the plants and how the Aranama Indians used them.

What about the park's other facilities? Besides screened shelters, tent sites, and hookups for trailers and RVs, it has a group shelter, swimming pool, picnic tables, and hiking trails. You can also fish on the San Antonio River.

THE TEXAS RANCHING BUSINESS GETS ITS START

This is where the Texas cattle business had its rudimentary beginnings. Well, perhaps it didn't just begin here in Goliad, but the whole area between Goliad and San Antonio was very instrumental in developing ranching. A lot of San Antonio missions had their ranches south of the city around Pleasanton and Floresville. And Mission Espíritu Santo's ranch was the biggest of all, extending roughly between the San Antonio and Guadalupe Rivers, almost as far north as San Antonio and Gonzales. See a map of it in the mission museum.

Note the Moorish points—or teeth—at the roof edge in this back view of Espíritu Santo church.

At its peak, Espíritu Santo had an estimated 40,000 head of cattle, not to mention a number of horses, mules, sheep, and goats. But cattle was the coin of the realm for the missions. Here at Espíritu, not only did the missionaries utilize the meat and leather, but they bartered hides and tallow for goods in San Antonio, the Rio Grande missions, and Saltillo.

Mission Indians were the ones who did the dusty, dirty work on this vast spread. They got on-the-job vaquero training whether they wanted it or not, because the two or three missionaries couldn't handle all the rough work plus their other duties. Most of the time the herds roamed on these huge grazing lands unbranded. But sporadic attempts were made in the fall to round them up.

HISTORY

Mission Nuestra Senora del Espíritu Santo de Zuñiga was founded originally in 1722 on the Texas coast near present-day Lavaca Bay, on Garcitas Creek in Victoria County.

The mission's long name has a tale behind it. It means Our Lady of the Holy Spirit of Zuñiga, and was partly derived from the Spaniards' original name for the great bay there: La Bahía del Espíritu Santo. Today, only a small inlet retains this title. The Zuñiga part honors some then-illustrious viceroy of New Spain. Later the mission and presidio were popularly called La Bahía, even after they moved to the present site.

Remnants of the original walls of a granary, which now houses the museum, can be seen in this photograph.

The mission-presidio complex was founded by the Aguayo expedition to discourage the French. That's why the exact spot of La Salle's failed colony was picked for its location. However, the Karankawa Indians proved cantankerous, and the mission and presidio had to move in 1726 to a spot on the Guadalupe River (at present-day Mission Valley, just north of Victoria).

Operations apparently went smoothly here, but the Spanish administration decided it needed a fortified settlement to guard the main roads from Mexico to San Antonio and East Texas and the Texas port at Copano Bay. Thus, mission and presidio were ordered to move to their present location at Goliad on the San Antonio River in 1749.

The local Aranama Indians seemed to take to mission life at Espíritu Santo, and at one time the mission housed as many as 300 Indians. Of course, the Indians were sly at adopting only what *they* wanted to of this new civilization cast upon them.

"To withdraw them from their pagan dances and diabolical mitotes," writes a visiting Franciscan bigwig, Fr. Solis, in 1768, "the ministers have introduced some Spanish dances. These dances have been taught with violin and guitar accompaniment, and the Indians have learned them very well. For such performances they wear a special dress . . . and very gaudy, and use palms, crowns, masks and ayacastles. As a result they have partly forgotten their mitotes and pagan dances. I say partly, because when the ministers are not watching them they go off to the woods, and there hold their dances. . . ."

Espíritu's first structures were made of wood and adobe, but gradually stone buildings replaced them, and by 1777 a new church was dedicated.

Unlike most of the missions, Espíritu couldn't seem to get an irrigation system going for some reason and lost some of its crops in dry seasons. Perhaps the San Antonio River was too low in its banks at this point.

As the mission system declined, Espíritu closed later than the rest, in 1830. But prior to this, the whole place had begun to deteriorate. In 1812, for instance, the Spanish forces added to the mission's wear and tear by headquartering at Espíritu while fighting the Gutierrez-Magee Mexican revolutionists that took over nearby La Bahía presidio. One little skirmish nearby was called "The Battle of the White Cow" because it all started when an insurgent tried to corral a cow outside of the fort.

In later years, from around 1848 to the Civil War, the mission grounds were used first by the Hillyer Female Institute and later the Presbyterian's Aranama College for men. At one time, the people of Goliad generally referred to the mission as the "Aranama Mission" until more recent years when the original name has been reapplied. So don't be confused by the seemingly different names.

By the time the mission's land was deeded to the state and made into a state historical park in 1931, most of the mission was in ruins. Much restoration work was done in the 1930s, and then more in the 1970s. The Texas Parks and Wildlife Department now maintains Espíritu.

Mission Espíritu Santo

1	Church Entrance	10	Reconstructed Grill Window
2	Museum Entrance	11	Indians' Quarters
3	Foundations—Original Floors	12	N.E. Corner Bastion
4	Preists' Quarters	13	Nature Trail—Lime Kiln
5	Remnant of Original Wall	14	Forge
6	Cistern of Well was located here	15	Ruins of Living Quarters
7	Skull and Crossbones	16	Hearth
8	Foundations of Convento	17	Adobe-Walled Compund
9	Workshop Entrance	18	S.W. Corner Basin

ARCHEOLOGICAL DIGS AND RESTORATION

Very little of the Espíritu Santo compound was left by the 1930s when it became a state historical park. Only a small room on the north side of the granary (now where the museum film is) was still standing. The rest of the structures were much like the ruins of the old priests' quarters you see on the west side of the granary, and some were worse. But Humpty Dumpty *was* put back together again, this time using the Civilian Conservation Corps. The granary, church, and workshop were rebuilt, and the surrounding square walls partially restored and stabilized.

The skull and crossbones (symbolizing transitory life) was a typical mission motif.

Before and during all this, extensive archeological digs uncovered artifacts and foundations. Among the artifacts upturned were tools, door ornaments, arrowheads, brass objects, nails, spurs, horse bits, beads, and pottery shards. All are on display in the museum. Archeologists discovered that there had been a well on the north side of the church near where it connects to the granary. And they also found remnants of foundations for a convento, probably never completed, attached to the church's north side also.

Museum and Mission Workshop Exhibits

This is one of the better mission museums, with appealing and well-designed displays. Housed in what was the granary, it begins with a large model of the mission compound in the late 1700s.

Exhibits highlight artifacts gathered in archeological digs, plus photos, documents, and maps. History, restoration, archeological excavations, Indians, ranching, agriculture, mission life, and defense are some of the topics covered. There is an elaborately carved brass cannon from Presidio La Bahía, and an almost life-size replica of two men manning a corner bastion. A ten-minute color film about the Coahuiltecan Indians can also be activated by punching a button. There is also a small gift shop.

The Mission Workshop building, behind the church and granary, offers an exhibit on weaving and spinning. All this is designed to portray how the Indians learned eighteenth-century crafts at the mission. In the same building is a reproduction of the office of a *mayor domo*, the Indian convert appointed as overseer for the workshop.

Directions to Espíritu Santo

From the intersection of Highways 183 and 59 in Goliad, take Hwy 183 south about one-quarter mile. Goliad State Historical Park's entrance is on the right, and the headquarters office is just off the road. Park there and pay. Mission Espíritu Santo is not far behind, just a walk up the hill.

Touring Espíritu Santo

Usually the staff is limited, and you take a self-guided tour with the free map. But the museum exhibits are so well done and explanatory that it doesn't matter. The staff does give prearranged group tours, especially for school children who love the boom of the special live cannon shot demonstration.

Presidio La Bahía

Presidio Nuestra Señora de Loreto de La Bahía del Espíritu Santo

On Hwy 183 about three quarters of a mile south of Goliad • Museum Open 9 a.m. to 4:45 p.m. daily except Thanksgiving, Christmas Day, and New Year's Day • Adults $3; children $1 • (361) 645-3752 • W

Presidio La Bahía. The name alone seems to hint of provocative adventure and political intrigue. And well it might. This old fort was the site of enough authentic warring and violence to satiate even today's appetite for the bizarre. About 342 Texas men were executed here by the Mexican

The chapel looms at the left behind a corner bastion at the Presidio La Bahía.

There was plenty of room for soldiers to train inside the large walled-in square.

army during the 1836 Texas revolution, which in turn led to the "Remember Goliad" cry later shouted at the Battle of San Jacinto.

Colonel James Fannin and his men, captured in a nearby battle, were unceremoniously and coldly massacred while they were presidio prisoners of war at the orders of Texas' old nemesis, Santa Anna.

"It seemed the prisoners were told different stories," writes one of the survivors (a doctor), "such as they were to go for wood . . . etc., and so little suspicion had they of the fate awaiting them. . . . The sound of every gun that rung in our ears told but too terribly the fate of our brave companions. . . ."

Because La Bahía, renamed "Fort Defiance" during Fannin's stay, was the scene of so many skirmishes during the Mexican and Texan revolutions and because it shows the key, dual relationship of mission-presidio life in eighteenth-century Spanish Texas, the presidio is being included in this guide. It's also one of the nation's best restored Spanish forts and is unalterably intertwined with its sister, Mission Espíritu Santo, down the road.

It was La Bahía's job to protect this mission and the later one, Rosario. The presidio compound was built much like a mission one. In fact, it's difficult to tell the difference between the two. Both were constructed in a square with fortified walls surrounding a large, open expanse of land. Each compound had a church, and then quarters and offices were built into the walls. Only the use of these adjunct rooms and buildings differed. Where the mission harbored Indian dwellings and trade workshops, the presidio housed soldiers and military supplies. And each mission was supposed to be supplied with two or three soldiers of its own from the presidio, though this didn't always prove to be the case. Too, where the presidio had four corner bastions for defense, the mission might only have had two on opposite corners.

La Bahía is situated high on a hill, just south of "downtown" Goliad, about one-half mile beyond Mission Espíritu and just off the highway. The setting is placid here, except during weekends and summers when the state park fills up. It's an ideal spot for children to roam up the ramps to the corner bastions (gun emplacements) and survey the countryside as soldiers did during the Texas and Mexican revolutions. The bastion in the northwest corner by the chapel has an ancient cannon to further fuel youthful fancies about the exploits of combat.

Though the fort dates back to 1749 when it was moved here (it originally began in 1721 elsewhere; see "History"), it has been restored mainly back to its 1836 era when Fannin and his men took over the garrison and later met their untimely deaths.

Enter at the west wall entrance, which also doubles as the museum area. These rooms were once officers' quarters, offices, and arsenals. There are no slide shows, but there are good exhibits, which include artifacts from extensive archeological excavations made during the 1960s restoration.

This is about all there is to tour inside, except for the chapel (Our Lady of Loreto) in the northwest quadrant and the enlisted men's quarters and calaboza (jail) in the south wall. But you're free to explore the quiet square enclosure, grassed over, with a few trees and indigenous cactus plants.

FANNIN AND THE GOLIAD MASSACRE

Probably one of the more infamous characters coming out of Texas' fight for independence was Colonel James Fannin. He's the same fellow who refused to take his men from the Goliad garrison (alias Fort Defiance or La Bahía) to aid his compatriots at the Alamo. Though he made a half-hearted attempt to march to San Antonio, he aborted it a little too easily, just out of Goliad, blaming it on a broken-down provisions wagon.

That was enough fuel for detractors. But on top of that, his poor military judgment ended up getting him and his men ambushed at the Battle of Coleto Creek (sometimes called the Battle of Goliad), captured, and executed. Of course, Fannin isn't around to defend himself, but the facts don't put him in too pleasing a light.

After the fall of the Alamo in San Antonio, Fannin received orders from General Sam Houston to blow up the Goliad fort and fall back to Victoria where the Guadalupe River would provide a defensible barrier. He disobeyed. Some say he did so because of conflicting orders from the lieutenant governor, but others think it was because he was jealous of Houston. Whatever, he thought he could defend his position at Fort Defiance. Only after it was too late did mounting Mexican forces finally convince him retreat was the answer.

About seven miles out on the road to Victoria in retreat on March 19, 1836, Fannin ordered his troops to stop to graze the oxen, and General

(*Map courtesy of Presidio La Bahía.*)

José Urrea's Mexican forces surprised them. "Colonel Fannin had committed a grievous error in suffering us to stop in the prairie at all," writes participant Dr. Joseph Barnard. "We ought to have moved on at all hazards, and all costs until we reached the timber."

Additional enemy reinforcements caused Fannin and his men to decide to surrender if they could do so honorably. The able-bodied could have bolted for the protective trees but did not want to abandon their wounded. This surrender has been controversial ever since. The Texans claimed the terms were that they were to be treated as prisoners of war and the wounded cared for. The Mexicans, however, contended it was unconditional (or "discretion") surrender, and that they, the captors, could do with them what they chose.

At any rate, the Texans were herded back to Fort Defiance, and crowded into the chapel for several days. Unsuspectingly on Palm Sunday, March 27, they were marched out of the compound on another pretext and shot. "My God, boys, they're going to kill us," one of the survivors remembers someone saying. It is generally thought that Urrea instructed the prisoners be well cared for, but was countermanded by General Santa Anna. The wounded were shot in the compound yard. Fannin died from a shot in the head. About 28 survived by running, hiding, and swimming the river. A few others, such as surgeons, were spared. In all, 342 are thought to have been massacred, though the exact figure is hard to trace. A memorial on the spot where Fannin and his men were buried is about one-quarter mile southeast of the presidio.

HISTORY

La Bahía can thank its existence to La Salle, the French explorer who landed on the Texas coast in 1685 by mistake. He had been heading for the mouth of the Mississippi, but ended up establishing the ill-fated Fort St. Louis colony in Texas.

The Spanish couldn't tolerate the idea of French encroachment on *their* territory, despite the fact the new French colony was a failure. The Indians killed off most of them, and La Salle himself was bumped off by one of his own men. But nonetheless, Spain felt the threat was there.

Marques de Aguayo was dispatched to build a mission and presidio on the exact site of the destroyed Fort St. Louis. There is some disagreement on when the presidio was founded. Historical markers at the present Goliad site say 1722, but some historians think it earlier in 1721. It was originally named Nuestra Señora de Loreto de La Bahía del Espíritu Santo (Our Lady of Loreto of the Bay of the Holy Spirit) after the nearby bay. The presidio was inland about five miles on Garcitas Creek, in what is now Victoria County. Now the nearest bay is called Lavaca, and only a small inlet still retains the original name.

The Karankawa Indians weren't too hospitable, however, so the whole kit and caboodle moved in 1726 to a spot on the Guadalupe River (what is now Mission Valley, just north of Victoria). Despite prospering there for years, the mission and presidio were moved to the present site at Goliad

See for yourself what it was like to look over the countryside from a defending position, complete with cannon, on the northwest corner bastion.

on the San Antonio River in 1749 because the Spaniards decided it was necessary to guard the main road from Mexico to San Antonio and East Texas. Thus was the good hilltop location chosen for La Bahía—the better to see the countryside. It was also located strategically on the road between San Antonio and Copano Bay, the main Texas port at that time. Here the presidio became known as La Bahía. Apparently the old name of Nuestra Señora de Loreto, etc. was discarded except in naming the new chapel, which was called Our Lady of Loreto. There is a statue there today of Our Lady, said to date back to the original founding.

Things were seldom dull after that. Besides bringing clashes with the Comanches and Lipan-Apaches during the last half of the 1700s, the advent of the 1800s brought revolutionary skirmishes between Mexicans and the Spanish and later between Mexicans and Texans.

During the Mexican revolt (1810–1821), several armed expeditions (such as the Gutierrez-Magee and James Long and Henry Perry "filibusters") attacked or took over the fort. Then in 1835, the Texas volunteer forces took it over, and Fannin renamed it Fort Defiance. The ill-fated retreat and Goliad massacre soon followed in early 1836.

Do you wonder how the nearby town became known as Goliad instead of La Bahía? The Mexicans rechristened it in 1829 in honor of a revolutionary hero, Hidalgo, by using "Goliad" as an anagram, without the "H."

The clashes and marauding troops took their toll on the fort, and by 1848–1850 when it was leased by the city to Judge Pryor Lea, most of it was in ruins except for the chapel.

The Judge actually used the chapel as a residence for his family! John Russell Bartlett writes of visiting him in 1850, "After tea we ascended to the roof, to enjoy the cool breezes of the evening, and the beautiful landscape which there opens to view. After the moon rose and cast a deep shadow from the ruined walls . . . the scene assumed an aspect of peculiar solemnity and interest."

MUSEUM, ARCHEOLOGICAL DIGS, AND RESTORATION

Old 1880 photos of the fort chapel show the building still standing with walls intact, but the bell tower on its left front is collapsed. The rest of the compound appears in ruins. Apparently somewhere around the 1930s, the simple rock chapel was restored and its belfry reinstated. This rough-hewn rock edifice is not an elegant, rococo chapel. It has only a little sculptured stone at the entrance, with a single statue in a niche above. Besides the bell tower, a few octangular windows and Moorish teeth on the roof are about the only other distinguishing characteristics. Inside, however, a huge, colorful religious mural on the back wall of the homely altar backdrops the vaulted ceiling and wooden pews.

Although some earlier restoration and excavations were done in the 1930s, the bulk was done from 1963–67 with the financial help of the Kathryn O'Connor Foundation.

At this time, careful archeological excavations were tediously done before restoring the entire walled compound back to its 1836 condition. All the dirt within the square enclosure was dug down six to eight feet and sifted and recorded. Around 3,800 artifacts, including gun parts, locks, copper pots, cannon balls, farm tools, pottery shards, china, and spurs

Inside the compound, the exhibit area is at the left, where the officers' quarters and arsenal were.

were uncovered from nine levels of occupancy, spanning the Indian, Spanish, and Texan periods.

Many of these artifacts, plus historical maps, documents, photos, and a large Spanish colonial bell dated 1748, are displayed in the pleasant museum, housed in the west military quarters and serving as the official entrance. Exhibit topics include Colonel James Fannin, the Battle of Coleto Creek, General José Urrea, Indians, Fort Defiance, and ranching tools. One important finding of the digs was the location of the main gate in the center of the south wall, where barracks, prison, and guard rooms were.

La Bahía chapel still operates as a Catholic parish church, and the entire presidio is owned and operated by the Diocese of Victoria and supported by admission fees, donations, and gift shop sales. The gift shop offers a variety of historical books.

DIRECTIONS TO LA BAHÍA

From the intersection of Highways 183 and 59 in Goliad, go south on Hwy 183 approximately three quarters of a mile (or one-half mile beyond Mission Espíritu Santo). On your left is Presidio La Bahía, just off the road. To peruse the museum and the inside of the fort courtyard, go to the west entrance.

This ramp leads up to the northwest corner bastion, where the cannon is located.

TOURING LA BAHÍA

There are no guided tours for individuals. Just amble around at your own discretion. The museum staff will gladly field questions. Prearranged lectures are available for schools and groups.

EL PASO MISSIONS

That remote foreign province known as El Paso, hundreds of miles west of the rest of Texas civilization, claims to be part and parcel of Lone Star country. In fact, the El Paso upstart even audaciously asserts to be the *very* beginning of Texas colonial history. For years, some historians have ignored the dusty, mountainous domain to the west as if it were a black sheep relative and have annointed East Texas with the honor of having been the site of the state's earliest Spanish settlements. But East Texas wasn't.

Even before La Salle's ill-fated, brief sojourn on the Texas coast, Spaniards were pitching their tents in El Paso del Norte in 1680. The Pueblo Indians in New Mexico revolted that year and forced the Spaniards to flee south for their lives. They regrouped in the pass made by the Rio Grande long used by explorers and conquistadores to go through the mountains.

This El Paso del Norte (the name actually refers to Juárez, Mexico, before it became "Juárez" some years later and abdicated the name of "El Paso" to what is now El Paso) was where Spaniards had for years come through on their way north from Mexico to look for the rumored cities of gold farther north in New Mexico. Another mission, Nuestra Señora de Guadalupe del Paso del Norte, had already been founded (in Juárez) in 1659, and to this area the Spanish fled in 1680, forming more missions along the Rio Grande in 1682.

With the shift of the Rio Grande banks over the years, two of these missions, Ysleta and Socorro, and the San Elizario presidio chapel remain to this day on the Texas side. The missions differ markedly in looks and architecture from those in San Antonio and Goliad. They have more of an Indian or New Mexican look, well punctuated by the presence of the Tigua Indian Reservation (only one of two reservations in Texas) at Ysleta. Too, there isn't nearly as much to see at these missions, other than the churches, because the walled compounds haven't survived the years nor have the missions been turned into restored state parks. (However, the El Paso Mission Trail Association is actively working towards preserving the area's cultural and architectural heritage.) But there *is* the rare opportunity to see the Tigua Indian culture. After all the Tiguas helped settle and build the Ysleta mission, and of late, they have smartly cashed in on the tourist trade by creating an entertainment center at the same site where their ancestors lived in their adobe houses.

If you don't linger long at each place, you can probably drive to all three (missions and presidio chapel) and back from downtown in three hours, but I suggest you allow more time for meandering about San Elizario and the Reservation, with its restaurant and dance performances.

If you prefer to leave the driving to *them*, there is a commercial trolley tour of the missions in the summer. Contact the El Paso Convention & Visitors Bureau or the trolley company (see below) for information on costs and schedules (somewhat limited at this time). It leaves from the Convention Center. For information in general about the missions, contact the helpful El Paso Mission Trail Association.

THANKSGIVING, TEXAS STYLE

Not to be outdone by Yankees up east Plymouth Rock way, Texas now lays claim to having the first Thanksgiving. At least if El Pasoans have anything to say about it. And they do. Locals are now good-naturedly tweaking Massachusetts that, indeed, the first Thanksgiving took place, not there in 1621, but in the El Paso area on April 30, 1598, near the little town of San Elizario, southeast of El Paso. Forget about the usual November Thanksgiving, it's more like April in El Paso. They point to the Don Juan de Oñate colonist expedition back then that was headed for New Mexico from Mexico and stopped along the way at the Rio Grande river banks near San

Elizario. They'd been tramping through the Mexican desert and having to eat roots and berries and drink water from cactus plants, so naturally you can see they were kind of glad to hit the Rio Grande for a little R&R. After resting for a while, old Don Juan ordered everybody to put on their finest and celebrate a feast of thanksgiving. We don't know if they had dressing and all the trimmings and afterwards watched football on TV or not.

OTHER SITES NEARBY

Many sites abound in the area, such as the Indian pictographs at Hueco Tanks State Historical Park (32 miles northeast of downtown El Paso), Fort Bliss, and the older Guadalupe Mission in Juárez. (If you visit Guadalupe Mission, note that the old mission is the small white building attached to the south side of the newer cathedral.)

WHERE TO GET INFORMATION

El Paso Convention & Visitors Bureau

One Civic Center Plaza
El Paso, Texas 79901
(915) 534-0696 or (800) 351-6024

El Paso Mission Trail Association

One Civic Center Plaza
El Paso, Texas 79901
(915) 534-0677

El Paso-Juárez Trolley Co.

One Civic Center Plaza
El Paso, Texas 79901
(915) 544-0062

YSLETA MISSION

Mission San Antonio de la Ysleta del Sur (now called Our Lady of Mt. Carmel)

Mission: 131 S. Zaragosa at Alameda Street in El Paso
Open Monday–Saturday 8 a.m. to 5 p.m., Sunday
9 a.m. to 6 p.m. • Free • (915) 859-9848
Tigua Indian Reservation: Cultural Center is at 305 Yaya Lane, (915) 859-5287; Casino and restaurant at 122 S. Old Pueblo Road, (915) 860-7777. Casino is open 24 hours, but check ahead about other hours.

Native Americans have often been overlooked in some southwestern histories. If not ignored, their culture has, at best, been shunned in assessing contributions to the region. But not so at Ysleta. Not only is Ysleta thought to be Texas' oldest mission (along with sister mission Socorro down the road), but it's next door to an authentic Indian reservation. These Indians' roots go back to the very beginning in 1680 when Spaniards either "encouraged" or coerced the Tiguas to come along with them in settling this wild, remote outpost in the El Paso area, or El Paso del Norte as it was then called.

Of course, the Tigua Indian Reservation (or Ysleta del Sur Pueblo) is a rather urbanized one at this stage, surrounded by pavement and the humble old town of Ysleta, which in turn is swallowed up by modern-day El Paso. Nowadays, the Tiguas' mainstay is their modern entertainment center, which is in the New Mexican vein. Like other national tribes, they've turned to the gaming industry for economic survival.

If not cowboys and Indians, at least you can indulge in playing casino games at this reservation complex that is only about 14 miles southeast of downtown El Paso and easily accessible most of the way by IH 10.

Still, you can see traditional Indian dances, purchase Indian jewelry or pottery, or learn about their history at their Cultural Center, about a mile away from their casino/restaurant complex.

The entertainment center is within walking distance of the old mission in the same block where it all began back in 1680 in the original vicinity where the Spaniards and the Tigua Indians fleeing from the Pueblo Indian revolt in New Mexico settled.

Unfortunately, Ysleta Mission, established in 1682, lacks the pastoral setting of the San Antonio missions. None of the original square or compound, or even a facsimile of one, is intact. All that remains is the restored mission church, surrounded by acres of pavement, modest utilitarian buildings, and the Tigua center. This is due no doubt to the ravages of time, pragmatic use, and lack of funds.

What is left of the mission itself, the church building, is appealing architecturally in a way dissimilar to the San Antonio and Goliad missions. Ysleta has more Indian influence. It is void of decorative stonework at the entrance and is covered with white plaster, with its silver-domed bell tower as its most identifiable mark. The church is stark and sublime, yet harmoniously elegant, with a sort of vague Alamo shape on the facade above the roof line.

The church itself doesn't take much time to see, since the sanctuary is all that's open. But the reservation or pueblo offers more options. You can either whisk through the shops in the center or linger over lunch. Colorful Indian dances are offered on weekends. If you don't want to miss these dances, call ahead for performance times; generally there are several around mid-day. Then, of course, there's 24-hour gaming for high rollers.

The Tiguas also perform dances on traditional observance days throughout the year, including Christmas and New Year's Day. And on St. Anthony's Day in June, they perform traditional ceremonies honoring their patron saint.

The Ysleta Del Sur Pueblo Dancers have been the official Tigua dance group since 1972 and have performed at many places, not only locally, but on regional and national TV. The dancers are teenagers who do condensed versions of traditional dances that deal with harmony, nature, and the balance of their elements.

WHO ARE THE TIGUA INDIANS?

The Tiguas hail originally from the New Mexico area, and are part of the Pueblo tribe. But they suffered a primitive employment relocation when the Spaniards, fleeing the 1680 Pueblo rebellion in New Mexico, took several hundred of them with them to Texas. Men, women, children,

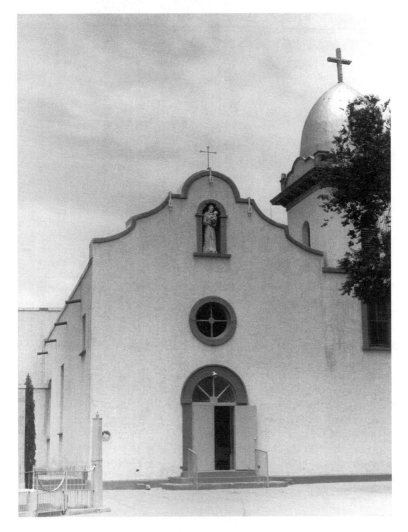

The dome of Ysleta's church bell tower is silver-colored. The church is the only building left of the Ysleta mission compound itself, and it had to be completely rebuilt around 1908 after a devastating fire.

A Tigua Indian performs traditional ceremonies outside Ysleta church.

and friars were massacred by the Pueblos rebelling against their Spanish conquerors in New Mexico. Finding retreat the best option at the time (they later returned and recaptured the area), the Spaniards took with them some Christianized Indians from the pueblo villages of La Isleta, Socorro, and Senecu in New Mexico to the El Paso del Norte area. These original pueblo names in New Mexico account for the corresponding town names at their new home, with only Isleta changed slightly to Ysleta.

The Tigua Indians (originally called "Tiwa," but later changed to Tigua to differentiate from their tribal brothers in Isleta, New Mexico) helped build the Ysleta mission and have lived in the area ever since. We first hear of the Tiwas from Coronado who set foot in New Mexico in 1540 looking for the fabled cities of gold. He encountered the Tiwas as one of the tribes living on the Rio del Norte (Rio Grande). During the cold winter the Spaniards demanded that the Tiwas give them clothing off their backs, and the Indians retaliated by running off their horses. After a truce, however, the Spanish burned a good many of the Indians at the stake—not exactly a charitable beginning for the conquerors and conquered.

Besides tilling the fields for and learning trades from the missionaries at Ysleta, the Tiguas served as scouts for the U.S. Cavalry and Texas Rangers in later years. One particular scouting incident was known as the "last scalp

to IH 10

Alameda-Hwy 20

Ysleta Mission

Zaragosa

Old Pueblo Road

Tigua Casino

restaurant

N

Socorro Road

dance." Some Texas Rangers had made their headquarters at Ysleta for protecting the area from the Apache Indians, and in January of 1881, the Rangers sent the Pueblo scouts out to find the Apaches near the Devil Mountains. After the Apaches were beaten in a surprise attack, the Tigua scouts halted about a mile outside Ysleta and camped, for such was their custom after a successful fight against the Apaches. Tribal members came from the Ysleta del Sur Pueblo to celebrate and honor the returning warriors and Rangers. For three days they feasted, wined, and dined. Thus the tale of the last scalp dance got its tag. Presumably some scalps were involved.

The Pueblo culture has also influenced our Southwestern architecture. And it's interesting how they built their flat roofs. The Indians spanned the space between adobe walls with horizontal beams (*vigas*) and covered these with smaller wood saplings (*latias*). Over these was laid a layer of straw, tules, chamiza, bark, etc., which prevented fall-out from the final six- to eight-inch dirt covering spread on the roof. But what happened when it rained, which fortunately wasn't too often in the Southwest? Well, by grading and pitch, water was directed towards roof drainage points, where an opening in the parapet and a canale (water spout) threw the rain free of the adobe walls. As might be expected, after a heavy rain families had to climb out on the roof to redistribute the earth covering and do some patch work.

When the Pueblos in New Mexico were given reservations during Lincoln's presidency, the Tiguas in Texas didn't receive similar land grants. And they weren't formally recognized as a Texas Indian tribe by the legislature until 1967. However, they did garner a lot of publicity at the Texas Centennial Folk Festival in 1936 by giving then-President Franklin Roosevelt an Indian headdress.

Today, the Tiguas occupy about 28 acres in the Ysleta area of El Paso, where their entertainment center, restaurant, administrative offices, and housing units are located.

The Tiguas have a traditional tribal government, with matters being resolved by the Tribal Junta (meeting of the people) and a seven-man Tribal Council, all headed up by a governor.

HISTORY AND RESTORATION

Texas' granddaddy mission has a muddled history that is a bit slippery to trace. But nevertheless, Ysleta is thought to predate other missions built in what is now the state of Texas. El Paso wasn't in the governing administration of the rest of Spanish Texas but was lumped together with New Mexico territory. This is one reason for the confusion in calling the East Texas missions the earliest ones in "Texas."

As said, Ysleta was founded in 1682 by the Spaniards fleeing and retreating from the Pueblo revolt in New Mexico (see the section on the Tigua Indians). Governor Antonio Otermin (from New Mexico) and Captain Alonso Garcia set up several missions and a presidio along the Rio Grande at El Paso del Norte, Ysleta among them. Franciscan Fray Francisco Ayeta helped with the establishment of the missions.

Presumably a hut served as the first temporary church. Then an adobe church was built by 1691 and lasted until the 1740 flood. The Tiguas helped build it. Originally, the mission was probably called Mision de Corpus Christi de los Tihuas de la Isleta del Sur (Corpus Christi means body of Christ, and Isleta del Sur means Isleta of the South, taking the name of the Tiguas' original pueblo, Isleta, in New Mexico).

In later years, the mission would variously be known as Mision de San Antonio (St. Anthony) de la Isleta del Sur, Nuestra Señora del Carmen, and now simply Our Lady of Mount Carmel. So the lady's many name changes are a bit difficult to keep up with.

Around 1744 an adobe church was built on the present site. And in 1851 the present church was built. In 1907 it fell victim to an accidental fire, either due to lit candles or to the sexton trying to eradicate the bats in the belfry having left some chemical overnight. Only a few walls, a statue, and a bell survived. The chapel was rebuilt by 1908, with Father Juan Cordova doing a lot of the work himself. Today, the church is shaped in the usual cruciform, fairly narrow and small, with the walls painted in creams and browns. The altar is ornate with many statues and a candelabra, and there are some mosaics on the flat ceiling. But it is still a workingman's parish.

In the mission's early years food was scarce, and compound residents had to scrounge for wild herbs and roots. But later the mission had fields of cotton, wheat, and grapevines. Yes, the good padres even brought grapevine cuttings from Spain, and the mission became renowned for its high quality of wine and brandy! The usual mission irrigation ditch, the acequia madre, supplied water. Ysleta wasn't secularized until much later than most of the other Texas missions—1881.

DIRECTIONS TO YSLETA AND THE TIGUA INDIAN RESERVATION

From downtown El Paso drive about 12 miles southeast on IH 10. Turn right on Zaragosa, going southwest about two and a half miles. The mission church is at the corner of Zaragosa and Alameda (Hwy 20). The Tigua Indian Reservation begins next door in the same block, though the Tigua Entertainment Center/Restaurant actually fronts on Old Pueblo Road. You can simply turn in left off of Zaragosa after passing the back of the church at Alameda. There is plenty of paved parking around the church and center.

TOURING THE TIGUA PUEBLO

The Indian Reservation, as mentioned earlier, encompasses several aspects. If you're game for casino games, the casino, or entertainment center, is open 24 hours, with the restaurant next door. But if you're more history minded, take a ride roughly a mile south to the Cultural Center on Yaya Lane, where you can take in the shops and see their native arts and crafts. Or check to see when the native dancing is scheduled.

"Beehive" ovens, or hornos, *are still used by the Tigua Indians.*

ANNUAL EVENTS

Many special days, most of them religious related, are observed by the Tiguas throughout the year, complete with their traditional dance performances. St. Anthony's Day is more special because St. Anthony is their patron saint. All are admission free. Below is a list of the days:

San Antonio (St. Anthony's Day)	June 13
San Juan (St. John)	June 24
San Pedro & San Pablo (Sts. Peter & Paul)	June 29
Santiago (St. James)	July 25
Santa Ana (St. Anne)	July 26
San Andres (St. Andrew)	November 30
Christmas	December 25
Inocentes (Holy Innocents)	December 28
New Year's Day	January 1
Santos Reyes (Three Kings or Epiphany)	January 6

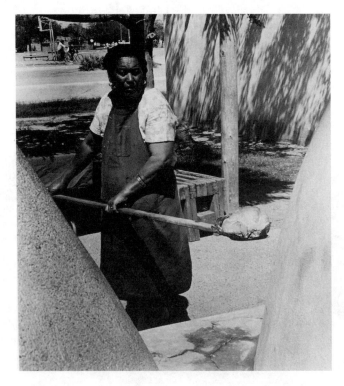

This Tigua Indian woman pulls bread from an oven. (Courtesy of El Paso Tourist and Convention Bureau.)

SOCORRO MISSION

Mission Nuestra Señora de la Concepción del Socorro (now called La Purísima)

On Nevarez Street at Socorro Road in town of Socorro, just southeast of El Paso • Open 8 a.m. to 4 p.m. Monday–Friday, call about hours Saturday–Sunday • Free • (915) 859-7718

From the side, it's easy to pass Socorro mission by and dismiss it as just another old stucco building found in the innumerable dusty little towns in the Lower Valley southeast of El Paso. Through no fault of its own, Socorro is somewhat of a let-down. Here's one of the oldest missions in Texas (it was founded about the same time as Ysleta was in 1682), and there's nothing much to distinguish it from the nearby weather-beaten structures of a poor community. The road crowds the mission on one side, and dusty pavement surrounds the rest. There is no pastoral green or walled-in square to buffer it like other restored Texas missions.

But after all, Socorro *has* survived, as many missions have not. And that's an accomplishment considering how the ravages of time often treat man's edifices. This poor parish and little town of Socorro have done well to just keep the church going, much less expend sparse funds for grandiose restoration. The town of Socorro itself is full of rare old adobe structures, and there have been attempts to marshal preservation efforts.

Mission Socorro's facade, which is white plaster over adobe, is quite unexpected and atypical of other Texas missions. It is stark and without

The Socorro church is vaguely reminiscent of the Indian thunderbird design. (Courtesy of James W. Ward.)

affectation, some say resembling the Indian thunderbird design. The wall bell tower with two bells sticks up in the front center and has a small cross on the top. The building is flat-roofed and has entrance doors that appear to be of more recent Spanish motel motif. But history-minded architects take a special interest in some of the original construction.

There is simply not much to see at Socorro, except the inside of the church, which takes only a few minutes, unless you want to investigate the old graveyard nearby. The church, which is not the original one and is estimated to have been built in 1843, is in the traditional cross shape, with many religious statues at the altar.

Of particular interest to architectural experts are the huge carved wood beams (or *vigas*) supporting the roof over the sanctuary. These were hand-carved by the Indians, and many were saved from the older mission when it was destroyed by the flooding Rio Grande in 1829. The Rio Grande was always shifting its banks, and this time it left the towns of Socorro and San Elizario on its north bank instead of its south one where they had been.

The mission does have one special event open to the public: its Fiesta Bazaar on one weekend in late September, honoring its patron saint, St. Michael.

HISTORY AND RESTORATION

Socorro's history is frequently elusive and frustrating because so many accounts differ. And as often happens, historians and archeologists update their opinions over the years as more data come to light. So keep this in mind in reading dates.

Socorro had the same pre-history as its sister mission, Ysleta, in the fall of 1680 when the Spanish fled the Pueblo revolt in New Mexico and retreated to El Paso del Norte.

Besides the Tiguas, the Spaniards also brought (how voluntarily we don't know) the Piro Indians from Santa Maria del Socorro in New Mexico. Governor Otermin and Fr. Ayeta founded Ysleta mission in 1682 and, a day later, the Socorro mission. Franciscan Fray Antonio Guerra said the first Mass under a cottonwood tree somewhere in the Socorro area, but not at the present mission site. A hut probably served as a temporary church. Not until around 1691 was a permanent church erected. After that several others may have been built and lost, due in part to the greedy Rio Grande which played havoc with the primitive mission structures. Another bad flood came along in 1829, and not only did the river wash away the church but it shifted its own course and left the mission site on the northern bank instead of the southern one.

This is when some religious objects and wooden support beams were saved, later to be put in the church built in 1843 at the present site. In about 1845, the mission fell heir to its statue of San Miguel (St. Michael) when a Socorro family donated it. Local oral traditions claim the more picturesque legend that an oxcart transporting the statue to New Mexico became mired in the mud at Socorro and thus the statue was destined to

The Socorro church is situated in the little town of Socorro, just outside of El Paso. (Courtesy of James W. Ward.)

remain there. But historians dispute this, pointing to church records that show it was donated by the Holguin family.

The belfry was added in 1847 and the transept in 1873. Italian Jesuits took charge of the mission from 1894–1915, and during a greater part of that time period, Father Juan Cordova supervised a lot of church improvements. Later the mission was reroofed, and in 1955, the exterior renovated.

Trying to ferret out the mission's official names along the way is as difficult as pinpointing dates. The historical marker and various histories each have their own versions. But a lot of missions have changed their names slightly over the years, and Socorro is no exception. It probably was called Nuestra Señora de la Limpia Concepción de los Piros de Socorro del Sur in the earlier years, and then changed to La Purísima Concepción del Socorro. Today, it's just known as La Purísima.

The University of Texas at El Paso did some archeological digs at a site approximately one-half mile from the present mission, and these ruins probably belong to an earlier church predating the present 1843 one.

Socorro is listed in the National Register of Historic Places and continues to serve as a Catholic parish church.

DIRECTIONS TO SOCORRO

If you are coming from Ysleta Mission and Tigua Reservation, just follow the Mission Trail signs and take the street bordering the complex on the south, Socorro Road (or Hwy 258), southeast for about two miles to Socorro. Turn left on Nevarez from Socorro Road. The mission is yards down on your right.

If you are going to Socorro mission from downtown El Paso, take IH 10 southeast about thirteen and one half miles. Turn right on Avenue of

Americas and go south to Socorro Road, where you take a left. Once in the town of Socorro, go left on Nevarez where the mission is located.

Annual Events

Weekend in Late September

Fiesta Bazaar—This is held around the feast day of Socorro's patron saint, St. Michael. It includes food booths, entertainment, and music. Free admission.

San Elizario Presidio Chapel

On San Elizario Road, just off Socorro Road, in the town of San Elizario (on the town square), about 22 miles southeast of El Paso
Open daily 8 a.m. until 5 p.m. in winter, until 6 p.m. in summer
Free • (915) 851-2333

This winsome white stucco chapel in the hamlet of San Elizario wasn't technically a mission, but it has traditionally masqueraded as one so long that it's being included in this guide. In actuality, the church was only a chapel for the local presidio.

But who cares about technicalities when you can visit this languid little town and its venerable town square, complete with gazebo and bench-sitting old-timers, reigned over by the adobe church? It's a journey back in time, only roughly 22 miles southeast from downtown El Paso. And you need drive only a few miles farther down Socorro Road from the two missions to take this in too.

The town of San Elizario is rich in local folklore anyway. It was the El Paso County seat and prior to that the headquarters of Spanish government. Even earlier, Oñate the explorer passed through here on his way to New Mexico in 1598. You can't get much earlier than that.

First Texas Thanksgiving

In fact, now San Elizario and the El Paso area are laying claim to having the first Thanksgiving in Texas, predating the Plymouth one in Massachusetts with their own Texas version. They say the first thanksgiving feast really was held near San Elizario in 1598 when that same Don Juan de Oñate made a pit stop at the Rio Grande after plodding through the desert of Mexico. On April 30, 1598, years before Plymouth's Thanksgiving, Oñate ordered his colonist and conquistador band to throw a feast of thanksgiving to celebrate their making it that far in the tough new world. Now El Paso and San Elizario celebrate this other Thanksgiving on the last weekend of April. San Elizario's town plaza comes alive with a festival.

Billy the Kid is also thought to have broken a friend out of the town's jail . . . one time he broke in and wasn't put into jail. And San Elizario was

The San Elizario Presidio chapel overlooks the somnolent town square of San Elizario.

the site of the Salt War in 1877, a local disagreement over the possession and price of salt dug from nearby flats. (Salt was in great demand before refrigeration.) Local politicians, landowners, and priests got embroiled in the controversy, which resulted in executions and murders and even the Texas Rangers surrendering to a mob!

The church, said to have been founded originally in 1789 as a chapel for a presidio here, is a pleasing sight in the more Indian architectural vein of Ysleta and Socorro. Chaste and natural in white stucco (over adobe), the chapel has no adornment, save the slender stained glass windows and wall bell tower in the center. The whole facade is shaped vaguely like the Alamo.

The church is in reasonably good condition, and inside, the sanctuary is much larger than most of the mission chapels. Much younger than the missions, this present church structure dates back to 1887 but has been remodeled. It is also much wider and in a square shape, with white walls inside and angels painted above the altar.

It takes little time to see the parish church, but dawdle a bit in the shady park square. Perhaps even brownbag a lunch there, or take in the jail or some nearby shops.

HISTORY

The history of San Elizario's Presidio Chapel is no less confusing than the nearby missions' histories, depending upon whether you consult historical markers or local data. Suffice it to say that when the Spanish retreated to El Paso del Norte in 1680 from the Pueblo revolt in New

Mexico, they needed military protection for their missions and a base from which to regroup and recapture New Mexico.

Thus, a presidio was established in the area, though it was shifted about to various Rio Grande locations over the years. Called Presidio de Nuestra Señora del Pilar y Glorioso San José, it was renamed San Elizario (actually spelled Elceario then, to honor the French saint St. Elzear) and moved here in 1789, when the chapel was begun.

By 1814 the presidio was abandoned, but the chapel continued to be used by local people. A flood in 1829 destroyed it, but still another chapel was built around 1853. The present chapel building dates back to 1887, with remodeling done inside in the 1900s.

DIRECTIONS TO SAN ELIZARIO

If making a tour of the missions, just continue southeast about six miles on Socorro Road (Hwy 258) from Socorro mission. After reaching the town of San Elizario, take a right on San Elizario Road. The chapel and park square are located about a block down. San Elizario Road is the next street after the junction of Hwys 258 and 1110.

If coming from downtown El Paso, and bypassing the missions, take IH 10 southeast, then take the exit to Clint and 1110 southwest to Socorro Road (Hwy 258) in the town of San Elizario.

ANNUAL EVENTS

Last Weekend in April

First Thanksgiving—The town and church of San Elizario celebrate, along with El Paso, what Texas calls the first Thanksgiving done in the United States by Juan de Oñate and his expedition in 1598 near San Elizario. Music, entertainment, food, and an outdoor Mass on Sunday. On the town square. Free admission.

OTHER MISSION SITES AND RUINS AROUND THE STATE

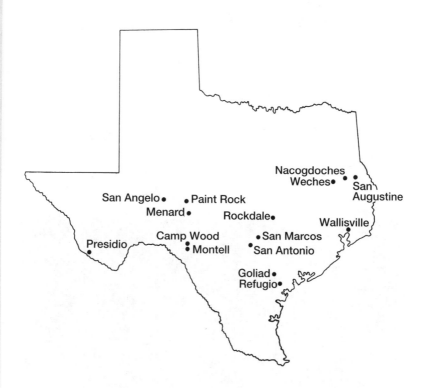

MISSION TEJAS

Mission San Francisco de los Tejas

On Hwy 21, just west of Weches in Mission Tejas State Historical Park
Camping and recreational facilities, historical structures • Church open
daily 8 a.m. to 5 p.m. • Park entrance fee ($2 adults) serves as admission
(409) 687-2394

Actually, this log church disguised as Mission San Francisco de los Tejas
is only a slight replica, and it's probably not even on the precise original
site. But why fret about such small matters? The first East Texas mission
was built *near* here in 1690 in these lonely, tall piney woods, and it's as
good an excuse as any to visit this beautiful area turned into Mission Tejas
State Historical Park.

Just outside of Weches, the park encloses about 360 acres of stately
pines with hiking and nature trails, plus a pond for fishing, a playground,
picnic area, campsites for tents, and hookups for RVs and trailers.

Keep in mind that Mission Tejas has gone through about as many name
changes as Elizabeth Taylor, so you have to keep alert when following its
history and various relocations. Ultimately, it ended up in San Antonio as
Mission San Francisco de la Espada (see San Antonio section).

This is a log replica of Mission Tejas built in the state park of the same name.

History

Mission Tejas began in 1690 because the Spanish were incensed at the idea of French explorer La Salle settling in their Texas territory. They retaliated by destroying the remains of his Fort St. Louis (La Salle had already been killed himself) and establishing two missions in East Texas. Mission San Francisco de los Tejas was the first one, founded by Alonso de Leon's expedition and Fr. Damian Massanet on San Pedro Creek a few miles south of the Neches River near present-day Weches. Designed to recruit the Nabedache Indians (whom the Spanish called *Tejas*, the natives' word for friends), the mission didn't fare too well. An epidemic killed off thousands of Indians, and the crops failed. The Indians blamed the priests and became threatening. In 1693, the priests were forced to abandon the mission, burning it themselves and burying the bells and cannon.

However, in 1716, the Spanish again felt threatened by the French and decided to reestablish missions in East Texas. Mission Tejas (now called Nuestro Padre San Francisco de los Tejas) was rebuilt about ten miles east of its original site in the Neche Indian village on the Neches River. War broke out between France and Spain, and again the mission was abandoned. In 1721 it was once again reestablished at the same spot, but under the name of San Francisco de los Neches!

Next, Spanish cost cutting led to decreased military protection, and three of the East Texas missions requested a change of venue. They moved temporarily to a site on the Colorado River in 1730, but ended up in San Antonio, on the San Antonio River in 1731, where Mission Tejas took on its last nom de plume, San Francisco de la Espada.

Park officials are the first to point out that the present log structure is not a true replica, that it would have probably been built of logs stuck side

Mission Tejas State Historical Park

Pond

Mission Commemorative

R Restrooms
◉ Residence
Ⓝ Nature Trail
Ⓗ Hiking Trail
⚠ Group Picnic Facility
⊗ Playground
◎ Trailer Camping Area
▲ Camping Area
✸ Headquarters
--- Park Boundary

Historic Marker
Rice Family Log Home

Weches

State Highway 21

North

by side in the ground, instead of parallel to it. However the site of the park was chosen because of the discovery of an old cannon believed to have been buried by the Spanish when they abandoned the mission. Located in Davy Crockett National Forest, the area became a state park in 1935, and the CCC (Civilian Conservation Corps) built a structure to commemorate the mission.

TOURING MISSION TEJAS

The log building is kept open all the time to visitors in the park, sometimes being used for church services and weddings. Take a self-guided tour with their map, or just pop in and have a brief look-see. It's at the opposite end of the park from the entrance on Hwy 21. Also in the park is an old log stagecoach stop, the Rice Home, built in the 1820s–1830s and moved here from its nearby setting.

Park Mailing Address:
Mission Tejas State Historical Park

Route 2, Box 108
Grapeland, Texas 75844

ANNUAL EVENTS

Easter Sunday

Easter Sunrise Service—Local ministers and music commemorate Easter. The fireplace usually burns in the background as the audience sits on the mission's log benches. The park entrance fee is waived for this event.

MISSION RUINS AND SITES

Most of the missions that still stand today, thanks to restoration and longevity, have already been covered in detail by this guide. However, there were innumerable more founded that didn't survive, either due to floods, hostile Indians, or simply erosion by time.

You'll see many historical markers all over the state locating former mission sites, but take them with a grain of salt. Historians are constantly updating dates and data, with newly uncovered documents, and this is the reason for discrepancies between the markers and updated information. Sometimes the marker may say a mission was located in a certain place when only a sub-mission (*visita*) or presidio or village was founded there. Sometimes it is the wrong site.

Unless you're a history aficionado, most of these sites aren't worth making a special trip to see. Some are just miniscule ruins hidden by weeds.

Others have no remains whatsoever—just a historical plaque. And sometimes, there is no plaque at all, because the actual site is unknown.

But if you happen to be in the area already, or are curious to know the various sites, here are most of the known ones.

APPROXIMATE LOCATIONS OF OTHER MISSION SITES

Presidio

For years historians thought that perhaps six missions were established in the Presidio area on the Rio Grande. Some recent researchers think it likely that only one real mission was started here in 1683–84 on the Texas side, and that several subsequent ones established about 1715 were merely sub-missions, or *visitas*. Though legend has Ft. Leaton being the original site of this mission, *El Apostol Santiago*, this has been debunked.

San Angelo, Paint Rock, Junction, or Menard

There are two possible mission sites in West Texas that historians speculate and differ on whether they were full-fledged missions. Some suggest it's possible that one was a much earlier, short-lived mission, referred to as the Jumano Mission, founded around 1632 in the San Angelo area. They think that a Spanish expedition that came across from New Mexico in that time period to recruit the Jumano Indians left a missionary there in 1632. If this short-lived endeavor was indeed to be considered a mission, this would make it Texas' earliest mission, earlier than the El Paso ones. In the same general West Texas area, another short-lived mission, *San Clemente*, was thought to have been founded around 1684 by the same Mendoza-Lopez expedition that earlier had started the Presidio one. Some researchers estimate the site to have been near Paint Rock or Junction. But others point to ruins (not those of the other mission Santa Cruz de San Saba mentioned below) near Menard as the location.

Weches

Another mission, *Santisimo Nombre de Maria*, was founded in this area shortly after the Tejas Mission in 1690, also nearby on the Neches River. A flood soon destroyed this one, and it had a short life.

Nacogdoches

Several missions were begun in this area in 1716. To the west was established *Concepción* (which ultimately ended up in San Antonio); to the north, *San José de los Nazonis* (which also ended up in San Antonio under the new name of San Juan Capistrano). And in the present-day area of Nacogdoches itself, *Nuestra Señora de Guadalupe de Nacogdoches* was also founded to serve the Nacogdoche Indians.

San Augustine

The site of *Nuestra Señora de los Dolores de los Ais* (1717) was located in the San Augustine area. The name means Our Lady of Sorrows of the Ais (Indians).

San Antonio

Besides the five surviving missions, an aborted mission *San Francisco Xavier de Najera,* was founded here in 1722 near where Mission Concepción is now. Whether it was technically a real mission is debatable. It was more like a temporary sub-mission of Mission San Antonio de Valero (Alamo) and never had any permanent structures. It only lasted a few years because Indian recruits dwindled.

Rockdale/San Marcos

Three missions were established in the Central Texas region near Rockdale between 1746–49. They were usually referred to as the San Xavier missions (*San Francisco Xavier de Horcasitas, San Ildefonso, Nuestra Señora de la Candelaria*) and have a hop-scotch history. Unsuccessful here, the missions moved subsequently to approximately near where San Marcos and New Braunfels are now.

Menard

The ruins of *Santa Cruz de San Saba* mission (1757) are east of town, and the presidio ruins are just to the west.

Camp Wood/Montell

The two missions in this area were named *San Lorenzo de la Santa Cruz* (ruins are just north of Camp Wood on Hwy 55) and *Nuestra Señora de la Candelaria del Canon* (site is a few miles south of Camp Wood on Hwy 55 at the present town of Montell).

Goliad

Another mission, *Nuestra Señora del Rosario,* was set up at Goliad in 1754 to convert the Karankawas who lived near its sister mission, *Espíritu Santo.* Although the Rosario site also belongs to Goliad State Historical Park, as of this writing, little has been done to enhance the scant foundation ruins. There is no sign indicating its whereabouts on the highway, but the site is about six miles west of Goliad on Hwy 59. It's not open to the public.

Wallisville

Again to discourage the French, a presidio and mission, *Nuestra Señora de la Luz del Orcoquisac*, were organized in this region on the Trinity River in 1756. "Our Lady of the Light" ministered to the Orcoquisac tribe, and its site is near IH 10 and Wallisville.

Refugio

Nuestra Señora del Refugio (Our Lady of Refuge), the last mission founded in Texas, was begun in 1793 near the juncture of the Guadalupe and San Antonio Rivers. It was later moved in 1795 to the Refugio area. Now a restored 1900s-era church sits on the mission's original foundations.

FRONTIER LIFE AND THE RISE AND FALL OF THE TEXAS MISSIONS

HOW THE FRANCISCANS CARVED OUT THE FRONTIER

Make no mistake, being a missionary wasn't for the weak or meek of heart. Those crusty Franciscan friars who settled the new world of New Spain and Texas must have been tough old birds, else they wouldn't have survived. Some of the missionaries didn't. If hostile Indians didn't get them, an epidemic or starvation was likely to. There were many hazards to the job of friar, and surely only the hearty lived to tell of it.

Take, for instance, the first mission in East Texas in 1690, San Francisco de los Tejas. In the first couple of years, some 3,000 area Tejas Indians died in an epidemic, and at about the same time one of the priests died too. The crops also failed, and the Indians blamed the missionaries for all their misfortunes. So they plotted to kill the missionaries, and the priests had to flee for their lives, burning and abandoning the mission.

Then when the friars reestablished the missions in East Texas in 1716, they didn't fare much better.

"Almost from the beginning, the fathers began to maintain themselves by the bread of tears and affliction," writes Fr. Espinosa in his *Cronica.* "The first trouble occurred when seven of the twenty-five soldiers who had been sent to guard the missions, deserted and abandoned us, at the same time taking along some of the animals destined for the use of the friars.

"After selecting the site of each mission, the missionaries assigned to them had to construct their little thatched dwelling unaided; and since no provisions were forwarded, abstinence commenced on the first day. Although it was not the season of Lent, the meals consisted of nothing more than a little purslane seasoned with salt and pepper. Once in a while the Indians would give us a little corn, beans of a certain kind, and some wild fruits, which served to distract rather than to appease our hunger. Rarely was a mouthful of meat available. . . ."

Of course, once the missions got firmly established and going, they became mini-cities and combination churches, forts, and schools, with an abundant Indian labor supply. Then the Indians really had to contribute to the work load, and had more to say grace over than they bargained for:

"Every day all the Indians recite in concert the text of the Christian doctrine . . . in the morning before work and in the evening after it," a report on mission Concepción in 1762 states. "Three or four times a week the ministers instruct the Indians. . . .

"The labor of the Indians is to plant the fields, look after the cattle, to water the crops, to clear away weeds, and to gather their grain, to erect their dwellings and other buildings . . . But they work with such slowness and carelessness that it is always necessary for some Spaniard to direct them. . . . Some work at weaving and in the forges, and others work as carpenters and bricklayers, in which trades instruction has been furnished them by the missionaries. . . ."

Naturally, we don't have the Indians' viewpoint on all this labor and enforced culture. There were probably pros and cons to the system, as far as the Indians were concerned. They gained skills, tools, and shelter, but had to adhere to the mores and religion of a foreign culture. More importantly, they had to relinquish their independence.

TYPICAL MISSION SETUP

To recap a bit, the typical mission compound included a church, friary for the missionaries, quarters for the Indians, a granary, and carpenter, blacksmith, and weaving shops. All of these usually connected and formed a walled-in square (or rough rectangle) around a large enclosed courtyard. At least two of the corners of the square would be fortified with bastions and cannons. Close by, an acequia would carry water from the river the Spaniards were always careful to build near. The mission farm would be adjacent to the square, and perhaps farther away there would be a mission ranch. As you can see, the missionaries had to be jacks-of-all-trades— teacher, carpenter, cattleman, architect, and preacher—to oversee all this diverse activity.

Most necessities—food, clothing, and leather goods—were produced by the mission itself. And cattle hides were used to barter for the goods that couldn't be made at the mission, such as guns, iron, and medicine.

Usually only two or three missionaries ran each mission, with maybe two soldiers for protection. But even the soldiers were sometimes capriciously withdrawn by the military. There seemed to be perennial bickering between the religious, military, and political factions in Spain's settlements, each accusing the others of being incompetent.

Most of the time there was a presidio (fort) in the vicinity to give added protection to the surrounding missions. But in belt-tightening times, Spain sometimes withdrew forts, and thus the safety of the missions was imperiled. This paucity of military protection frequently led to the missions' abandonment.

OVERALL HISTORY OF TEXAS MISSIONS

Earlier I detailed how individual missions evolved, lumping them together geographically as you might want to visit them. Now let's pull them all together and take a brief, overall look at the rise and fall of the Texas mission period in general.

First of all, in following the missions, remember they frequently moved from place to place when rivers flooded them out or some budgetary chieftain decreed they relocate. And often they changed names when moving, so that what may have appeared to be a new mission was actually an old one revived. Establishment dates also tend to be elusive, and historians periodically adjust them as more documents are uncovered.

So, it's difficult to pinpoint just how *many* missions were actually founded in Texas. How you total them up depends on your definition of a mission and whether you count a reestablished mission with a new name/location as a new one. Many heretofore thought-to-be missions were actually only sub-missions, or visitas, or villages. Some historians put the total number of missions in the thirties. But by counting the relocated missions only once and discarding some of those that researchers now feel were only sub-missions, a lower total in the twenties is possible. And this rough estimate is subject to change as academics continually update their research and opinions!

To reiterate, the first missions in Texas were not in East Texas, but in the West Texas region. A mother mission, Guadalupe, had already been formed in Juárez, Mexico, in 1659. And when the Pueblo Indians revolted against their conquerors in New Mexico, the Spaniards retreated to the El Paso area in 1680, establishing several missions in 1682, two of which ultimately ended up on the Texas side—Ysleta and Socorro. (And a few historians suggest that maybe the first mission in Texas was really a brief one they call Jumano, set up in the San Angelo area in 1632 when a Spanish expedition came there from New Mexico to minister to the Jumano Indians.)

From here history is a bit sketchy. For years academics estimated that perhaps six missions were then established in the Presidio area, farther down on the Rio Grande, beginning in 1683–84. Now some recent researchers think that only one mission, El Apostol Santiago, was founded around 1683–84. The others were more likely only submissions or visitas when they were established around 1715. A fort and mission were also founded on the Mexican side, and the whole area at that time was called La Junta de los Rios.

The same Mendoza-Fr. Lopez expedition that had come out of Juárez (the El Paso area) to found the mission at Presidio also wandered out into the interior of West Texas in 1684 to establish what may have been another mission, San Clemente. Historians disagree as to whether it was an actual mission and even where it was located. Some say it was near Paint Rock or Junction. Others say that it was more likely near Menard.

Then in 1685, the Frenchman La Salle upset the Spanish applecart by sailing accidentally to the Texas coast while looking for the mouth of the Mississippi River. His ill-fated Fort St. Louis colony on a creek off Lavaca Bay near Victoria didn't last long, and he was killed. But the settlement set off rumbles in Spanish officialdom.

Immediately, expeditions were sent out to destroy his camp and discourage the French by settling in East Texas. The de Leon expedition established mission San Francisco de los Tejas near Weches in 1690, among what the Spaniards called the Tejas Indians. Soon after that, in the same year, a short-lived mission, Santisimo Nombre de Maria was started nearby. The Spanish had to abandon Mission Tejas because of threatening Indians and hardships, and for the time being, Spanish colonization of Texas lay in the doldrums. Some missions were formed on the other side of the Rio Grande in Mexico, however.

Then France started making noise again in the Louisiana-Mississippi area, and Spain reacted reflexively by going back to East Texas in 1716–17 to reestablish Tejas and five more missions in the area (Concepción, Guadalupe, and San José de los Nazonis in the Nacogdoches area, Dolores de los Ais in the San Augustine area, and one in Louisiana) plus a presidio (near Nacogdoches).

A few years later, it dawned on the Spanish that they needed a halfway station between their settlements on the Rio Grande at Eagle Pass (San Juan Bautista) and their East Texas ones. The way was a long trek for men and supplies through hazardous territory. This led to the settlement on the San Antonio River and the birth of the Alamo (San Antonio de Valero) and a presidio there in 1718. Later another mission, San José, would be started in 1720. Hence the evolvement of the El Camino Real (King's Highway, also called the Old San Antonio Road) from Eagle Pass through San Antonio to the Nacogdoches area.

Meanwhile back in East Texas in 1719, the missions were having their usual troubles, such as crop failures and sickness. And too, France and Spain had gone to war. When a few French soldiers appeared in the area, the Spanish fled to San Antonio, abandoning the missions. Like an instant replay, the Spanish *again* returned in 1721 and reestablished the missions, adding a presidio near the Louisiana mission.

Around this time in 1721–22, near the coast where Fort St. Louis had been, part of the Aguayo expedition, which had just gone to East Texas, veered to the coast and set up another presidio-mission duo, which eventually became known as Mission Espíritu and La Bahía presidio. This was the same pair that later moved to the present town of Goliad. Again, this settlement was designed to discourage the French and protect the Spanish's coastal landing area.

Administrative cost-cutting soon closed down the East Texas presidio. As you can see, Spanish officials never could quite agree on whether the settlements in Texas were worth the expense, and they constantly wrote up reports closing or opening them. Anyway, three missions (Concepción, San Francisco de los Tejas, and San José de los Nazonis) requested a geographical transfer for safety's sake and ended up eventually in San Antonio in 1731. San José de los Nazonis took on the name of San Juan Capistrano.

Meanwhile, the Catholic church felt compelled to Christianize and civilize the plains Indians. In the end, this would prove to be an unwise move. The hunter tribes were more warlike than the fairly peaceful agricultural tribes the missionaries had dealt with before. But undaunted, the church established several missions in central and west Texas to accomplish this goal. In general, these met with *deadly* failure.

Beginning around 1746–49, three missions were started near Rockdale (northeast of Austin), with an accompanying presidio. They were called the San Xavier missions because of their location on what was then called the San Xavier River (now San Gabriel). Their actual names were San Francisco Xavier de Horcasitas, San Ildefonso, and Nuestra Señora de la Candelaria. Apache raids and the murder of one of the missionaries led the missions to be moved farther south to the San Marcos River near where San Marcos and New Braunfels are now.

The facts are not entirely clear, but in their zest to Christianize and placate the Apaches, the church/state decided in 1757 to establish a mission and presidio in West Texas on the San Saba River at what is now Menard. Spain wanted to explore purported mineral lodes in the area and open up closer communication with its New Mexican settlements. The Apaches, however, were not amenable to being civilized at this newly named mission, Santa Cruz de San Saba, and the marauding Comanches were even less so. The Indians killed several people at the mission, including two padres. So much for this missionary attempt.

The friars, however, were a determined lot. They soon founded two missions in 1762 on the Nueces River near the present towns of Camp Wood and Montell. Here the two missions took on the names of San Lorenzo de la Santa Cruz and Nuestra Señora de la Candelaria del Cañon (sound familiar?). Although the Apaches at least congregated there, they never really acquiesced to the work schedule and discipline, and the missions bit the dust in a few years.

After starting the San Xavier missions, Spain started worrying about the French again in 1756 and decided they needed to put a mission (Nuestra Señora de la Luz del Orcoquisac) and presidio closer to Louisiana on the Trinity River near present-day Wallisville and Anahuac. (The mission was abandoned, after not much success, around 1771.)

Around this time, 1749–1755, several visitas, or sub-missions, were created in South Texas along the Rio Grande. They didn't have resident missionaries and would be visited by one periodically, rather like a preacher traveling the circuit.

In 1754, another mission, Nuestra Señora del Rosario, was erected to serve the Karankawas near the La Bahía presidio and mission (at Goliad). And in 1793, a little to the south closer to the coast, the last Texas mission to be organized was Nuestra Señora del Refugio. From then on the Spanish shifted their main efforts farther west to California. By the 1790s, about the only missions still surviving were in San Antonio, La Bahía, and El Paso, plus the one in Refugio. Those in the "Texas" district were officially closed or secularized (turned into regular parish churches, with the lands and tools divided among the resident Indians) around 1792–94, except for the ones near La Bahía and Refugio. These operated on until around 1829–31. But actually the San Antonio missions (except the Alamo) were only *partially* secularized until 1824.

Why did the mission system decline? Well, for one thing, perhaps the time had come for it to disappear in the sunset. While historians may disagree on just how successful the friars were in Christianizing the Indians, the mission-presidio system had fairly well served its purpose of settling and conquering a foreign land and its people—at least from the Spanish viewpoint. Spain had been able to use native labor to build churches and villages, and at the same time some skills and material goods were imparted to the Indians. The padres had also tried to treat the Indians' sicknesses and souls. And in all fairness, when the missions were secularized, land and equipment were parceled out to the resident Indians.

One decisive blow that accelerated the missions' demise was an official decree around 1778–80 that declared that all unbranded cattle belonged to the government. The Spanish crown had decided that Texas was a drain on the royal pocketbook, and that cattle was the only resource to tap. Indeed, cattle were the main source of the missions' income, and naturally most of the cattle weren't branded. This dealt a final economic blow to the already tottering mission system.

BIRTH OF THE TEXAS CATTLE INDUSTRY

Speaking of cattle, this brings to mind another chief contribution of the missions—the cattle industry. Spaniards like Cortez brought cattle and horses over with them when they came to Mexico, which then infiltrated northward to Texas. The expeditions establishing the missions also carried cattle and livestock with them, so consequently cattle ranching spread.

This was particularly so in the San Antonio-South Texas area. All the San Antonio and Goliad missions had ranches, with Espíritu's being the largest. It had an estimated 40,000 cattle at one time. The ranches were not necessarily adjacent to the missions. For instance, Espada's ranch, Rancho de las Cabras, was located about thirty miles southeast of San Antonio, near what is now Floresville. There are still a few ruins left today at the site (near Hwy 97), but the area currently is not open to the public. The ranch headquarters could be quite large themselves, including quarters for the Indian vaqueros and perhaps a chapel. Las Cabras had 26 residents at one time. Many of our cowboy and ranching terms, such as rancho, bronco, hacienda, chaps, poncho, and corral, come from the Spanish.

RESOURCES FOR LEARNING MORE ABOUT THE MISSIONS

BOOKS AND BOOKLETS

There are many books on Texas mission history—some scholarly and effusively detailed, some brief booklets. Here are just a representative few that should be available at libraries or bookstores:

Ashford, Gerald, *Spanish Texas*, Jenkins Publishing Co., The Pemberton Press, Austin and New York, 1971.

Bolton, Herbert E., *Texas in the Middle Eighteenth Century*, first published in 1915, then in 1962, reprint by the University of Texas Press, Austin, 1970.

Burrus, Rev. Ernest J., booklet on El Paso missions, Historical Cultural Commission of the Catholic Diocese of El Paso, 1981.

Castañeda, Carlos E., *Our Catholic Heritage in Texas*, 7 vols., Von Boeckmann-Jones, Austin, 1936–1958; reprint, Arno, New York, 1976.

Daughters of the Republic of Texas, *The Alamo Long Barrack Museum*, printed by Taylor Publishing, Dallas, 1986.

Eastland, Tom, and Fred Armstrong, *The Goliad Massacre*, a booklet, Victoria, Texas, 1974.

Eaton, Jack D., *Excavations at the Alamo Shrine*, Center for Archeological Research, the University of Texas at San Antonio, Special Report No. 10, 1980.

Guerra, Mary Ann Noonan, *The Missions of San Antonio*, Alamo Press, San Antonio, 1982; *An Alamo Album*, San Antonio, 1981.

Habig, Marion A., O.F.M., *The Alamo Chain of Missions*, Franciscan Herald Press, Chicago, 1968, revised 1976; *San Antonio's Mission San Jose*, 1968;

The Alamo Mission: San Antonio de Valero, 1718–1793, 1982; *Spanish Texas Pilgrimage: The Old Franciscan Missions and Other Spanish Settlements of Texas, 1632–1821,* 1990.

Jackson, Jack, *Los Mestenos—Spanish Ranching in Texas, 1721–1821,* Texas A&M University Press, College Station, 1986.

Junior League of San Antonio, *The San Antonio Missions National Historical Park, a Guidebook,* 1986.

Leutenegger, Benedict, O.F.M., series of translations of mission documents and diaries for the Old Spanish Missions Historical Research Library, San Antonio, 1973–81.

Long, C. J., *1836, The Alamo,* a booklet of the Daughters of the Republic of Texas, 1981.

Lord, Walter, *A Time to Stand,* Harper and Row, 1961; Bison Book paperback, University of Nebraska Press, Lincoln, 1978.

Morrow, Herbert C., *The Mission Trail: History, Architecture, Cultural Heritage, and Historic Preservation of the Lower Valley of El Paso, Texas,* a report for West Texas Council of Government, 1981.

O'Connor, Kathryn Stoner, *Presidio La Bahía,* printed by Von Boeckmann-Jones Co., Austin, 1966.

Perry, Carmen, (translator and editor), *With Santa Anna in Texas, A Personal Narrative of the Revolution by José Enrique de la Peña,* Texas A&M University Press, College Station, Texas, 1975.

Ramsdell, Charles (revised edition by Carmen Perry), *San Antonio, A Historical and Pictorial Guide,* University of Texas Press, Austin and London, 1959, 1976.

Torres, Louis, *San Antonio Missions,* Southwest Parks and Monuments Association, Tucson, Arizona, 1993.

University of Texas Institute of Texan Cultures at San Antonio, Samuel Nesmith, principal researcher, *The Spanish Texans,* a booklet, 1981.

LIBRARY RESEARCH RESOURCES

Listed below are some libraries with good resources for researching the missions further:

Daughters of the Republic of Texas Research Library is located at the Alamo in San Antonio. It contains material on the history of Texas, in particular the Texas Republic period. Books, documents, maps, photos, periodicals, newspapers, clippings, and family papers are available for research.

Old Spanish Missions Historical Research Library at Our Lady of the Lake University is at 411 S.W. 24th Street in San Antonio. It specializes in the Spanish colonial period of Texas history, particularly the Franciscan missions. There are microfilmed copies of archival documents from Mexico, Spain, and other countries, plus maps, slides, and photos. The library has printed a documentary series of translations of some of this material. Open mainly by appointment.

Institute of Texan Cultures is at HemisFair Park in San Antonio. Besides a Spanish colonial exhibit on the ground floor, it contains a reference library on Texas history and folk culture, plus a collection of historic photos.

University of Texas at Austin library system has a large collection of originals and transcripts of old documents from Spanish and Mexican archives. See also the *Texas State Library* in Austin.

INDEX

ABOUT THE AUTHOR

Nancy Haston Foster, a Phi Beta Kappa graduate of the University of Texas at Austin, is a full-time writer living in San Antonio. She is the author of *Lone Star Guide to San Antonio* and a contributor to the San Antonio section of the *Lone Star Guide to Texas.*